"Today's challenges and pressures can make life very difficult at times. I have never seen biblical principles for tackling those challenges presented in such a logical, relevant, and compelling way. This book offers an eye-opening perspective about how the choices you make shape your future. It makes you think about your life and relationships in a whole new way. I don't think this is a book you will read once and put on a shelf. It's more like a reference guide—a handbook for successful living that you will refer to over and over again. I appreciate the author's willingness to be so transparent about his life experiences in order to help others."

—L. SMITH, Minneapolis

"Beginning with the provocative title that Mr. Prescott readily admits is aimed at himself, this engaging narrative pulls you right into an exploration of the author's life journey that results in a series of deeply insightful conclusions. The book leads off with an intimate memoir as Prescott unfolds for the reader the evolution of his understanding—of the world, of his life, of his reactions to people and events. We feel like we are experiencing in real time the discoveries that gradually unfolded to him over the span of decades.

Those discoveries, prompted by two rather extraordinary and sobering not-of-this-world interventions, lead Prescott to a series of realizations and that he distills to a list of imminently practical, yet profoundly useful life principles. What sets this work apart from a "how-to" self-help book is the candor and perspective with which those principles are delineated. The author sprinkles thoughtful Christian insights throughout his list, but he does so in an unconventional manner without ever preaching. While some of his points have been made before, of course, this work flows from a refreshing perspective based on the author's genuinely grappling with his personal life experiences. I found *Managing Your Inner A**hole* to be stimulating and remarkably applicable to me despite my very different life experience."

—NICK WARNER, PH.D.

"Ben Prescott has written a remarkable book about his life-long journey to find meaning in life and manage his dark side. He presents a series of life lessons that we can all benefit from. At times they are funny, at times sad and at times it gives you the feeling you are reading your own diary. The life lessons are direct, helpful for anyone wanting to improve their outlook on life and provide ample reminders that in the struggle between your good self and your inner a**hole, the one that wins is the one you feed."

—JOHN FISHER
President, rethinking IT, Chicago

"Every couple should be required to read this book before they get married. They should read it again each time they have a child. They should reread it on every anniversary and each time their kids have a birthday. This book is that important!"

—ANONYMOUS

"Having grown up in an environment that looked good on the outside, but was inwardly incredibly dysfunctional, Ben Prescott presumed that what he had been exposed to was normal. His subsequently skewed perspective manifested upside-down values and left him lacking the tools needed to properly navigate and nurture personal relationships.

In this candid, highly enlightening book, the reader takes an up-close and intimate journey through personal and business scenarios which force some serious self-examination. Through Ben's courage and transparency and all that he ultimately learned and incorporated into his life along the way, we gain hope and the certainty that each one of us is capable of conquering our shortcomings and cultivating a requisite, healthy emotional intelligence.

As a mother, I sincerely hope that my young adult children and many more like them, now at the threshold of finding accomplishment in business and fulfillment in strong close relationships, will absorb these life-lessons and thereby avoid potential pitfalls that delay the development of skills and awareness needed for a truly successful life."

—IRENE DUNLAP
Co-author, *Chicken Soup for the Soul* book series

"He shares the lessons he's learned—often the hard way—with humility. He holds up a mirror that helps us see ourselves more realistically. He discusses truths he's learned about people, relationships, and life, truths that can set us free to live out a healthier and more satisfying story. I wholeheartedly encourage you to accept B. W. Prescott's invitation to manage your inner a**hole. You won't regret it."

—BETH RUSSELL, Orange County

"This is simply an amazing book. It leverages a life's worth of interesting, tragic and often shocking events to create a rule-set for a happier, more productive life. The story of what happened is hard-hitting and impossible to put down, while the lessons learned demonstrate years of thoughtful reflection that result in guidelines that are both intuitive yet original. This book will make you thankful for the beauty and the ugliness in your life. It feels like the author genuinely wants to connect people who've struggled with life's more gritty challenges in order to help break the silence and move towards a collective recovery. Whether you consider your own path to be particularly difficult or particularly easy, this book offers an unusually blunt yet articulate perspective that will leave you feeling hopeful, connected, and empowered."

—DAN BARNETT, San Francisco

"I began reading this book thinking I might find some new tools for improving my behavior, but I discovered there are really two books here. On the surface this book offers thirty-two lessons for improving emotional intelligence. While I'm absolutely sold on the idea that these lessons need to be embraced, practiced continually, and passed down from generation to generation, it wasn't the lessons that I found most compelling. What was most compelling for me was the incredible impact this man's life could have on his reader. Ben presents a tear-jerking story of a beautiful disaster. This second book is a story of real hope that defines a clear, logical and incredibly practical path for anyone facing challenges in their life. His explanation of how we all have a choice in how we manage our lives and navigate the circumstances we can't control is profound. I have never seen anybody lay out a step-by-step roadmap for improving your behavior and life before. There is hope, you just have to choose it, and when you do you'll change the trajectory of your future. Brilliant!"

—COLE ANTHONY, San Diego

Managing
Your
Inner
A**hole™

An Unusual Education in the Fundamentals of
EMOTIONAL INTELLIGENCE

by

B.W. PRESCOTT

SECOND BLESSING MEDIA

The Story Is True. The Names Are Fictitious.
This is true story. It is not a work of fiction. However, for reasons that will become obvious as you read, most of the people referenced in these pages do not wish to be identified. This book deals with events that have been very painful for those involved. Because of this, I have changed all names and have either avoided the sordid details of the events or made minor changes to those details to protect the identity of the participants. For the same reason, I am publishing this book under a pseudonym. I am concerned that if I were to use real names, others might be able to identify the innocent third parties who were affected by these events and force them to publicly relive their experiences.

Dedication

To my wife, my son, and my daughter—the
three greatest gifts of my life. Thank you for
staying with me on this journey,
and thank you for all you've taught me.

With all my love and undying gratitude.

Table of Contents

Preface

There are two types of people in this world: those who admit that they can, at least on occasion, be a complete jackass—and those who are liars. The corollary to this truth is that the more vehemently you deny the fact that you can be an ass, the more unequivocally you confirm that you are one. The sad reality of the human condition is that we've all got a part of our personality that we would prefer never saw the light of day. Some of us manifest these behaviors more often than others, but we all have the capacity to behave badly.

I've come to visualize this aspect of myself as having its own persona. He's an obnoxious blowhard. He never used to shut up, but over the years I've gotten better at rendering him mute. He's given me more bad advice and demanded I make more bad decisions than all the stockbrokers I've ever met. He's ignorant, petty, vindictive, cruel, selfish, and mean. He's also scared and pathetic, but it took me years to realize that. At any rate, this is the entity I refer to as my "inner a**hole." Yours may be similar; on the other hand, it may be different. Being male, I shall refer to this character in the masculine.

Although I readily admit that the title of this book is intentionally provocative, I do hope no one takes offense. I'm not trying to be crass or crude or—as seems so common these days—to get a cheap laugh by pandering to the lowest common denominator of our society. I'm simply being candid and frank: I'm acknowledging the obvious that we so often try so desperately to deny. I'm calling out the detestable within myself—and within all human beings—for what it is. I'm laughing at my own failings and limitations, and I'm encouraging others to do the same.

I believe that we all have a part of our personality that is arrogant, defensive, mean, petty, selfish, vindictive, and just plain dumb. I don't like that part of me, and I bet you don't like that part of you either. While I don't think it likely that we will ever banish such personality traits from ourselves, much less our population, I do believe that we can minimize these less desirable qualities and cultivate more constructive behaviors—if we choose to. I also believe that we will have a better chance of making such changes if we work together, hold each other accountable, and encourage one another along the way. So, as you read this book, please read it as an open, albeit lengthy, invitation to join a movement that is dedicated to improving the emotional intelligence of America one a**hole at a time.

Before I get to that invitation, I want to make clear why I'm undertaking this project.

First, they say you never learn material like you do when you have to teach it. The act of writing all this down has been quite an education for me. It has also been humbling, because there isn't one principle that I share in this book that I don't regularly violate. Just so you don't think I'm suggesting, "Do as I say and not as I do," please know that I actually try very hard. I'm just calling myself on my own BS, admitting my hypocrisy up front, and getting it on the table early. I would like to state for the record that the first inner a**hole I'm trying to manage is my own!

Second, as I approach sixty, I'm increasingly aware of the fact that I won't be here forever. So I would like to share a written record of the things that I have found crucial to the cultivation of a healthy mental, emotional, and spiritual life. I hope to help cultivate your emotional intelligence. I'm not suggesting that the ensuing list of lessons is complete—or even completely accurate—but I feel I can safely say that it's not without merit.

Third, I've come to realize that, over the last thirty-five years, I've had the benefit of an unusual education and career. Having traveled from academia to business, having been a member of management teams that started, built, and sold four companies, and having advised and worked with literally hundreds of other organizations from across the US and Europe, I have met some wonderful and uncommon people who have introduced me to ideas and practices that I probably would not have encountered in a typical work environment. At the risk of sounding full of myself, I think it might be worthwhile to share a bit of what I've learned.

Fourth, these lessons I share are things that I've learned the hard way, and I don't want others to have to do the same. My ignorance of, and my failure to embrace, the principles I describe in this book have caused me an enormous amount of pain. My life has been much harder than it had to be. I've wounded people I didn't want to wound. I've impeded my own progress in ways that were completely unnecessary. I've not only shot myself in the foot, I've done so repeatedly. Talk about being an A**HOLE! As one of my grad school professors once told me, "It's the little things that will kill you." Well, these are all little things, but they can make a very big difference in the quality of your life. The earlier you begin to understand these concepts, the bigger the difference they can make in your life.

Fifth, when I was about forty-five, I started to realize that my mission in life was not to seek my own advancement. Up until that point I had been looking to make *myself* rich, successful, influential, etc. I came to realize that my mission was to make *others* successful. I have come to see myself as the catapult on the aircraft carrier and those I care about as the jets. My job is to throw them as fast, as far, and as high above me as I can. The higher they soar, the more successful I'll be. My goal is to prepare those who come after me for the journey of their lives and to help them make the most of the trip. I'm a servant, not a star. If I achieve anything of significance in this life, it will be because of the support I offer, not because of something I've done.

Finally, I'd like to give you a sense of hope—something you can hold on to during the darker times of your life when you might need it. I'd like to share two rather extraordinary experiences. The first happened to me when I was twenty-six; the second, when I was forty-three. Both of these were blatant interventions in my life, and I do not believe that either of them originated in this world. These encounters were like two black holes that unexpectedly appeared in my personal universe. Their gravitational pull redirected my trajectory in a way I never could have anticipated. However, instead of throwing me off course, they surprisingly put me on the right one. The first encounter confirmed for me that the life we see on this earth is not "it" and that God is real. The second experience helped me to appreciate what life is about and to begin to understand what we are to "be about" while we're here.

In the interest of full disclosure, I want to alert you to three things. First, there's probably not an original thought in this entire book. All I've done here is synthesize and interpret divergent ideas that have been around for thousands of years. Brighter people than I came up with this stuff; I just borrowed it from them and pulled it all together. Second, the lessons I'm sharing are based on my personal experience. Everything in this book is filtered and presented through the perspective of a male entrepreneur in his late fifties who has a strong commitment to faith in God and philanthropic service. Third, I'm going to be candid and unvarnished.

Do not expect me to be politically correct, and not being a theologian, I will deal with some theological concepts in an unconventional way.

In the pages that follow, I'm going to explain several principles that I firmly believe form the foundation of emotional intelligence. These are the fundamentals, the basic building blocks, the rules of relational life. I'll occasionally refer to them as "secrets," because—as obvious as they seem now—they sure weren't evident to me initially. And I don't think I'm alone in this. From what I've observed, a lot of people have never thought about these ideas—or at least have never fully appreciated them.

I believe that embracing these principles can help anyone be more successful. I believe these principles can help us cultivate character and compassion. I also believe we can all be happier—and we can all have healthier relationships—if we appreciate that the quality of our life has much less to do with the environment we inhabit than it does with our perspective on that environment.

I hope my ensuing arguments are persuasive. But in the end, of course, it's your decision: you can take what I'm about to say or leave it. If I achieve nothing else, though, I hope I cause you to think, and to seriously consider the invitation I extended above.

Introduction

This book covers a journey of forty years. It's about the lessons I learned to right the ship of my life after doing my level best to sink it. I'll explain a bit about where things went wrong, but I won't spend much time on that. I think it's far more useful to explain the ways I made the wrongs right.

This book is divided into five sections. The first is a case study, a summary, and a timeline of my journey to date. The last four sections, respectively, describe lessons or principles I've learned and "tools" I've acquired for dealing with my self, other people, relationships, and life over the course of that journey.

I've learned something interesting about my inner a**hole over the last forty years. The timing of his appearance is predictable. He always shows up when I'm tired, threatened, frustrated, scared, angry, or confused. He's my knee-jerk reaction to a situation when I either don't know what to do or don't have the time to think through my response. I've found that the more tools I acquire for handling such situations, the more confident I get, the less frustrated, angry, and frightened I become, and the less often I behave like an ass. I would like to think that there's a methodical way to acquire those tools. At the very least, I would like to explain the logic I've used to acquire mine.

A couple of years after I left grad school, one of my professors who happened to also be my boss and mentor left academia to work directly for Jack Welch, the then-current rock star CEO of GE. In his new position, my professor became the first executive in the world to hold the title "Chief Learning Officer." As the name implies, it was his job to facilitate GE's learning, growth, and adaptation. During his tenure with GE, the company grew phenomenally and was widely regarded as one of the best-run corporations in the world. Prior to that time, when I was studying with him, he often used a simple illustration that I never forgot. It was a great analogy for what he and Welch would later do at GE, and it clearly explains just how easy it can be to improve performance. It's all about fixing the little things that will kill you if you get them wrong.

My professor's performance improvement story goes like this:

> *I don't play a lot of golf. But I know that when I'm about to putt, if I look down and see that there's a stick between my ball and the cup, if I move the stick, I'm going to have a much greater probability of sinking that putt.*
>
> *Now, in an organization where you have a lot of people all doing relatively the same type of work, one of them will usually figure out how to "move the stick" faster than the others do. Your job as a*

manager is to identify that person, ask them what
they did, and then share their secret with everyone
else. When the entire organization becomes
aware of and has adopted the new technique, the
average level of performance will improve, and the
organization will be better off. That's when you
start looking around for the next stick.

I think that approach can work as well in our personal lives as it can in a corporation. Think about it. We're all doing the same job—it's called life. And some of us figure out how to "move sticks" faster than others do. If we can capture those lessons and share them, I think we can significantly improve the quality of our lives. That's why I've spent the last thirty years taking notes whenever I figured out how to move a stick or I saw someone else do it. This book is a summary of that education. All the lessons that follow represent sticks that got moved.

In my travels, I have been surprised to find that our mental prowess or intelligence quotient (IQ) seems to have much less to do with our ability to "move sticks" or live a successful life than I would have thought. I know plenty of very smart people who are not— by any definition—successful. I've found that one's emotional intelligence quotient (EQ), on the other hand, seems to have a great deal to do with whether a person becomes successful. That's why this book is dedicated to exploring the lessons, principles, and tools that I have found to develop EQ. Before I dive into describing those lessons, though, I think it's important to clarify what I'm talking about when I speak of being or becoming successful and, perhaps, more importantly, to define what I am *not* talking about. And that's where I'll start.

When I use the word "success," I *am not* talking about what I believe many people will immediately presume. My definition of success does not pertain to creating financial wealth; amassing power or material goods; gaining notoriety, fame, or prestige; realizing personal or professional accomplishment, advancement, status, or title; or achieving interpersonal (whether professional, personal, or sexual) conquests. In short, I'm not referring to the standard materialistic definition of success.

Ironically, I've found that when people pursue the kind of emotional and behavioral success that I'm about to describe below, they invariably attain material success as well—at least to the degree that they desire such success. I, and many others, have found that material wealth often follows as a natural consequence of emotional wealth. Contrary to the protestations of the ethically challenged and morally bankrupt who try to excuse or justify their unscrupulous behavior by claiming it's the only way to get ahead, nice guys, good guys *do not* finish last. In the end, good guys *always* finish on top!

Therefore, when I talk about success in this book, I'm focused on the success of your soul and spirit, of the better angels of your nature winning the battle over your worst demons. I'm talking about the triumph of your intellect, reason, and humility over your raw emotion, instinct, arrogance, and desire for self-preservation and advancement. I'm talking about your being able to live with a profound, daily attitude of gratitude for the people and intangible gifts of your life, instead of with a perpetual dissatisfaction over the things that you don't have and a burning, unrelenting desire for more. I'm talking about your capacity to give of yourself to others; to consciously choose to give love and extend grace and compassion to those who may have done nothing to deserve it; to forgive the unforgivable and restrain from judging or condemning others who might well deserve it. I'm talking about your capacity to intentionally choose responsible and constructive behaviors that advance your cause—rather than to unconsciously default to instinctive behaviors that impede it. I'm talking about you developing both a ravenous curiousity that seeks out such constructive behaviors and a willingness to readily adopt the solutions you discover. I'm talking about your ability to live directed by your life's purpose—rather than being controlled by your past mistakes or current circumstances. When I talk about success, I'm talking about, first, your philosophical commitment to live by exemplary moral, ethical, and intellectual standards and, second, your behavioral consistency in living in such a way that you not only uphold those standards, but serve as a role model and inspiration for others to do so as well.

What I am defining as success is a very lofty ideal that I do not come close to being able to achieve. But it is a goal that I'm working toward. Sadly, it's a foregone conclusion that your inner a**hole, like mine, is going to escape into the open every now and then. It happens to all of us. My objective for this book is to help you minimize those events and to provide you with some tools so that when your inner a**hole does escape, he (or she) doesn't take over.

PART ONE

A Case Study

The older I get, the more convinced I am that life is nothing more than a giant classroom. This part of the book is a summary of the class I've taken. It's less than a biography, but more than a bio. The only reason I've included it is to provide context. You see, I don't think it's right to share a set of ideas for cultivating emotional intelligence without first sharing the premise upon which those ideas are based. So let me start by explaining the experiences that shaped the worldview I've come to embrace.

Every person alive has a worldview. Whether they've articulated it to themselves or not, they still have some perception of or theory concerning what the world is about and of their place in this world. Our worldview gives us our bearings much like a map and GPS help us determine where we've been, where we are, and where we're going. Our worldview helps us figure out where we fit into this life, and it helps us to come to grips with the trials and tribulations that we all face.

In my experience, people's worldviews fall along a surprisingly simple continuum that runs from completely random chaos (there is no God, no Heaven, no Hell, everything that has happened has happened by chance, and each of us is alone in the universe) to meticulously predefined order (God made the universe, He's in total control, and I'm just a pawn of fate). I've known people at both ends of this spectrum who were kind, decent, ethical people. And I've known people at both ends who were miserable bastards.

As nice as it would be to follow the simple rule that says, "Believers in God are good and nonbelievers are bad," I think such logic is inappropriately simplistic and dead wrong. I don't think the real issue is whether you believe in God; I think it's how you choose to respond to that decision after you make it.

When you start to evaluate the principles I share later, I want you to understand the foundation upon which those principles are based. So, in this section, I will briefly explain my worldview, how I came to hold it, and why I've chosen to put that view into action the way I have.

CHAPTER 1

A Quick Trip
From Bad To Worse

I was born in Southern California at the peak of the baby boom, 1957, into a white, middle-class family with deep New England roots and a bloodline leading straight back to the *Mayflower*. We were Christian by default—meaning we weren't Jewish, Muslim, Buddhist, or Hindu. My paternal great-grandfather, who had died forty-five years before I was born, had been a Methodist minister. As far as his descendants were concerned, that fact alone determined their religious beliefs. In my family (as with countless others across the centuries) a faith in and a relationship with God were not things that you needed to personally think about or come to individually. They could be inherited like eye color, and their benefit extended through simple association with any ancestor who had once given the matter some thought.

Education was very important in my extended family. My father had earned his bachelor's degree before I was born. My mother finished hers when I was five. Both of them ended up with master's degrees, and my father later pursued his doctorate.

As important as education was, image and making a lot of money seemed to be even more important. The pursuit of wealth was a constant theme that I recall from even my earliest memories: the topic largely consumed the conversation at family gatherings. Since both of my parents were teachers, who didn't make a lot of money, this subject posed a real problem for my father. He was the poor man on the totem pole, and his family—especially his younger brother, who was a successful entrepreneur—never let him forget it. Over time, the insecurities and the sense of inadequacy this created in my father festered. You can't let steam build up in a pressure cooker indefinitely and get away with it; so too with a man.

When I was very young, my parents weren't around much because they were working during the day and going to school at night. But after my father finally finished graduate school, when I was about six, he still wasn't around much at night. In fact, he was gone all the time. He said he had a lot of night meetings. He also claimed to have a lot of flat tires; it seemed as if he had one a week. In fact, just about every time he had to pick my little brother or me up from school, he was late— and always for the same reason. Those damn flat tires!

When you're seven years old, you just accept what your dad tells you. Now, if you ask me why my mother accepted his explanations, that's another story. My father was a very handsome man from an upper middle-class family. He was very conscious of these facts, and he frequently attempted to play them to his advantage. My mother was not unattractive, but as a teenager she had suffered with severe acne that had badly scarred her face. She was extremely insecure about her appearance and was always very sensitive about the disparity in their looks. Adding to her insecurity were the facts that her father had died when she was a teenager, her mother was crippled from polio, and she had come from a working-class family of limited financial means. I think my mother thought herself very lucky to have landed the husband she did, and she was willing to make certain accommodations to keep him. If I add in the obligation of caring for two young sons and consider the prospects of a single mother in the sixties living on a teacher's salary, I begin to wonder whether she was simply afraid to ask too many questions. I think she so desperately wanted to believe that her marriage was okay that she actively denied any sign or suspicion that her husband might be involved in something he shouldn't be.

My family life changed for both good and bad in '67. On the positive side, my father got a job as a principal, which meant more money and more prestige. On the downside, my brother began to develop behavioral issues. In '68 we moved about forty miles south of where we had been living. In '69—whether as a result of the move or the approach of puberty and adolescence—my brother's behavior deteriorated markedly. In the months and years that followed, getting him to school and keeping him in class became a near impossibility. When he did go to class, his behavior in the classroom was extremely disruptive. He was—and is—a brilliant guy, but his intellect only seemed to fuel and enable his increasingly sarcastic, condescending, and contemptuous outbursts at all those around him.

The late sixties and early seventies were not a time of great enlightenment when it came to behavioral health, particularly regarding children. If a child misbehaved back then, it was assumed to be a direct result of the parents' inability to discipline that child and therefore either a moral or intellectual failure on the part of the parents themselves. Given the facts that my brother and I both attended schools in the district where my father was now a principal and that my brother was now becoming a daily visitor to his principal's office, it didn't take long for my father's phone to start ringing. It also didn't take long for the buzz to start among the upper administrators in the district that one of their new principals couldn't control his own kid. For my father, this was just more pressure in the pot.

As the seventies rolled on, the situation deteriorated. My brother's issues intensified. The medical model was applied, but to no benefit. Tests revealed some minor anomalies, but nobody knew what they meant or what to do about them. Counselors were consulted, but none helped—and none lasted. To make up for this, I tried to play the role of the good kid. I got good grades, followed instructions, and internalized my growing stress. (That strategy proved to be not particularly successful, as I was eventually hospitalized with a bleeding ulcer.)

My father, once proven to be incapable of correcting the situation, simply checked out. His evening meetings, which had significantly abated following our move, were suddenly back with a vengeance. Now, too, his weekends were booked. On the rare occasions when he was home, he was either extremely moody or sitting in a catatonic trance. He started to have flashes of anger and, for the first time, became physically violent.

On July 12, 1974, a bomb exploded in my family that inflicted collateral damage that lasted for years. Lives were ruined. Jobs were lost. Arrests were made. Bullets were dodged (literally). Relationships were severed. One person committed suicide. One was later murdered. Generally, all hell broke loose.

Turns out, my dad was a sex addict with an entrepreneurial streak. From my perspective, the shock and sense of betrayal were almost unimaginable. It was a real Jerry Springer moment. There had been hundreds of women and countless orgies. He and several of his "friends" had been making their own porn movies in which some of them starred. They recruited local prostitutes to "flesh out" the casts. They used my father's school's video equipment to shoot, edit, and replicate the tapes. They were working with some very shady people to distribute their products. And, worst of all, they were running the entire operation out of my father's elementary school. It was a nightmare waiting to happen.

This operation had apparently been going on for a couple of years before someone got careless. A video was accidentally left in a school VCR where the PTA president discovered it. That was the beginning of the end. Today my father would be in jail, and the story would be all over the news. Back then, though, scandals like that were made to quietly disappear.

My mother had known about one of my father's early affairs, but it had happened years before, and she thought that episode was behind them. She had no idea what he was up to until the day the dam broke and the entire story came flooding out. Honestly, I think very few people knew what he was doing. He'd covered his tracks pretty well.

When confronted with the facts, however, my father's social-climbing, Puritan family—who outwardly appeared to be very pious—closed ranks and flatly denied the reality of my father's addiction. When push came to shove, they were much more interested in preserving their public image than maintaining their moral standards. Every attempt I made to gain clarity about the situation, or to confront obvious contradictions, was met with a condescending "You just don't understand" or "You're just not mature enough." Finally, it dawned on me that they were frauds and that their perfect façade was merely an elaborate hoax. I had been lied to since birth.

What I didn't realize then—but certainly understand now—is the fact that nothing threatens the ecosystem of addiction like the innocent who insists on asking the obvious question "Why is that elephant in the living room?" Those who wish to maintain the status quo of the ecosystem will go to incredible lengths to deny the elephant's existence, even to the point of blaming or even punishing the child who sees it. I was such a child, and once I realized what was really going on, I became enraged.

This is the point in my life when I could have really used a trusted mentor. Someone to let me know that what I thought was a solution to my pain was, in fact, not a real solution. Unfortunately, I didn't have anyone like that to turn to—so I took a bad situation and, for the next eight years, diligently proceeded to make it even worse.

What passed as wisdom to an extremely immature, brokenhearted seventeen-year-old was stupid beyond measure. Although I didn't articulate my thoughts this clearly at the time, my rationale was threefold, fairly simple, and straightforward: First, I assumed that if my family said that something was wrong, then it must be right, and vice versa. Second, I assumed that the world is fair and I was entitled to fair treatment. If I were treated unfairly (however I defined *unfairly*), I was within my rights to demand something better. Third, I assumed that if I could not understand the logic or perspective of another person, then that person's intent must be malicious. I concluded that all such persons were untrustworthy and dangerous and that they were trying to manipulate or otherwise harm me. In such situations, I concluded that the best defense was a strong offense, so I viciously attacked these people with the self-righteous rage of a victim determined never to be a victim again. In each of these three cases, my assumptions were wrong, but it took me years to realize that fact.

At seventeen, I thought that my new perspective made total sense and that the resulting behavior set me free. The good news was that I did stop being the victim of others. The bad news, however, was that the behaviors I adopted caused me to victimize others. I became a trap in which I caught myself.

What I didn't realize at the time was that I had embraced the childlike logic that assumes that if a strategy works in one situation, it must work in all situations. The strategies I adopted made, at best, very little sense when applied to my dysfunctional family. They made no sense at all when applied universally to all other people, situations, and circumstances. I will return to this discussion in greater depth later, but for now just let me note that it is extremely dangerous to leap to conclusions and assume that one size fits all.

Armed with my new set of social tools (sledgehammer, ax, chainsaw, and dynamite), I pursued my new lifestyle with tremendous zeal. I did what I thought was best, which included, among other things, largely breaking ties with the past. There was a period of several years during which I hardly spoke with my family, and I abandoned all but one of my friends. During that time, I graduated from high school early, went to work full-time, started drinking and using drugs at an alarming rate, grew a chip on my shoulder that was bigger than my feet, rejected religion entirely, and threw away anything that looked like a moral compass. I changed nearly overnight from a fairly sweet kid into a complete bastard.

I was filled with rage. I erupted at the drop of a hat. My tirades ran from minutes to hours. The more inebriated I was, the less provocation was required to set me off. I was a mean but articulate drunk. I had an extremely high tolerance for drugs and alcohol that allowed me to maintain the outward appearance of sobriety while I was actually heavily intoxicated. That capacity kept me out of jail on more than one occasion, but it did not serve me well. Nearly forty years later, my friends still talk about my more outrageous outbursts.

On the positive side, during this same period, I was accepted into a somewhat prestigious university and earned two bachelor's degrees in four years. I also worked forty-plus hours a week for three and a half of those four years to put myself through school. Since my father had completely abandoned us financially, I not only paid for my education, I also occasionally helped my mother pay the mortgage. She had gone back to school to get her master's degree, hoping to use that advanced degree to make more money so we didn't lose our home and she could finish raising my younger brother. To drown my sorrows, I drank and drugged and somehow wound up as the president of my fraternity.

The real danger that emerged and became ingrained in my soul and character during my undergraduate years was not the partying. It was my attitude toward those people I didn't understand and my unhealthy, near-total consumption with work. Work became my escape. It was my true addiction. It was nothing for me to go two, sometimes three days without sleep. I only drank and drugged to numb my emotions so I could ignore my life and focus on work.

Being a workaholic was how I got my rewards, where I found my praise and sense of self-worth, and how I was able to wall off the unpleasantness of human relationships, which had, at least so far in my life, proven to be so messy, so disingenuous, so untrustworthy, and so horrifically painful. Although I could not see it or at least not admit it to myself at the time, I was terrified of people. I feared that, if given the chance, they would always hurt and betray me.

For me, work was an addiction that seemed both safe and constructive. It was an unrecognized problem that I would contend with for the next thirty years, and one that would interfere with and do tremendous harm to almost every personal relationship I would have during that period. The only advantage of my being a workaholic was that it was my highest priority addiction. When the time came for me to abandon first drugs and then alcohol, it was remarkably easy for me to do so because, by then, I had come to the realization that drugs and drink were getting in the way of my ability to work.

These realizations came later, however. In the prelude to these epiphanies, I had to discover for myself what so many have discovered before me: the human body wasn't designed to ingest an unlimited amount of drugs and alcohol or to continually burn the candle at both ends. By mid '77, the start of my junior year of college, I began exhibiting symptoms that significantly impacted my work. Random midday blackouts, sky-high blood pressure, an irregular heartbeat, the occasional inability to speak, weight gain—just the basics. A few of these scared me enough that I stopped using drugs. Alcohol was safer—or so I thought—and legal, so booze became my sole focus.

It was at about this time that I entered into my first truly serious relationship with a woman. There had been girlfriends before, but this one was different. In spite of all my rebellion against my family, I found myself secretly thinking that this girl would elevate or establish me in their eyes. As much as I claimed to hate them, I craved their acceptance. My girlfriend was at once all that they represented and all that I professed to loathe. She was everything I wasn't, and vice versa, yet for some strange reason, we were attracted to each other.

Image was everything to her. She was the homecoming queen, the stage actress, the socialite. Truth was not an absolute construct for her. It was situational, malleable—a story that could be adjusted at will, should either expediency or objective require it. She wanted people to admire her, but failed to realize that honesty, integrity, and character are prerequisites for true admiration.

Meanwhile, intellect was everything to me. I was the wickedly sarcastic, would-be genius you didn't want to cross. Civility and respect were unnecessary social contrivances for me. They served no purpose other than to window-dress the harsh realities of my dog-eat-dog existence. I was still convinced that in the pursuit of success, a strong offense is the best defense. I wanted people to fear me, but failed to realize that winning through intimidation is always temporary, self-isolating, and personally destructive.

As the years went by, my girlfriend and I each cultivated our dysfunctional personas. Playing those roles made us happy, at least at the time. It also kept us safe from other people and from our own insecurities. Regrettably, we were both willing to do almost anything to maintain our individual happiness and safety. This is not a recipe for the development of a healthy human being. Nor was it a recipe for developing a functional relationship—and over the next six years, no one would ever accuse us of having one.

In 1980 I entered grad school. I was still in what was becoming a very troubled relationship, and I was perfecting my drinking skills by consuming one to two gallons of vodka, tequila, or whiskey each week. I would get up every day at 5:30 AM, go nonstop with school and work until 11:30 PM, drink heavily for two to three hours (or however long it took me to come down and pass out), and then start the cycle all over again in the morning. Running on three to four hours of sleep a night, I earned my master's in fifteen months. I also entered a doctoral program after the first nine months.

I was an anomaly in that program from the outset. At twenty-three, I was the youngest student in the group by seven years. I was more than able to keep up intellectually, but psychosocially I was a mess. My lack of emotional maturity was catching up to me. My lifestyle and coping mechanisms were serving me very poorly.

Toward the end of the second year of my doctoral program, things began to fall apart. A few of the faculty and older students tried to talk to me, but I didn't see them as allies. My ill-advised strategy of assuming that everyone I didn't understand was a mortal enemy worthy of a full nuclear response caused me to push away the very people who were trying to help me. Imagine a guy who walks around with a handgun shooting himself in the foot all day—and imagine that anytime he isn't shooting himself in that foot, he's shoving the other foot in his mouth. I was that guy. I was my own worst enemy.

I could go on and on with one illustration after another about the deplorable state of my emotional intelligence during my late teens and early twenties. But I don't think that would be productive. I don't want to turn this into an inventory of my sins. I just want to establish that I have a firsthand understanding of what it's like to be a first-rate a**hole. I have been the angry young man. I know of which I speak. When it comes to screwing up, I like to think that I once set a pretty high bar. I know what it's like to be stuck in a ditch. And I know that it's only an unmerited act of providence that saved me from being stuck there forever.

At the end of my eight-year emotional slide came the coup de grâce: after two years of relational turmoil, my girlfriend (after months of literally pleading) convinced me that the way to fix our problem was to get married. Whether I agreed out of guilt, obligation, fear of being alone, or outright stupidity, I'll never be absolutely certain. However, I do know this: adding a marriage into the mix for someone with my emotional deficiencies was a recipe for disaster.

That disaster arrived in mid '82, when I was twenty-five, and it lasted a couple of years. It was the most painful chapter of my life, but it became the wake-up call that saved me.

CHAPTER 2

One Very Weird
Wake-Up Call

The older I get, the more interesting I find the fact that a relatively small number of brief events are, for many of us, our defining moments. These moments, in many cases, determine the trajectory of our lives, the people we become, the lessons we hold dear, and the cornerstones of how we view the world. There have been a handful of such events in my life—moments when I have gotten a very tangible sense that the physical world in which we live is not the totality of the universe we inhabit. I know that the story I'm about to share will sound insane to many people, but I've got to share it anyway.

Over the years I've had a few glimpses "behind the curtain" that have profoundly shaped my perspective on life. While I have no idea what is actually back there, I'm absolutely convinced there is a lot back there. I don't know whether this is Heaven, but I suspect it is. All of these glimpses have been memorable, but two were positively life-changing. I will explain the first now and the second in chapter 6.

To pick up where the last chapter left off, I was twenty-five and still in graduate school when I married my long-term girlfriend. The wedding was a mistake that never should have happened. Our marriage started to fail within weeks, and it disintegrated in a fireball over the course of the next year. The fault was every bit as much mine as it was hers, perhaps more so. On top of my marital troubles, my temper and arrogance had caused me to leave my doctoral program in the middle of the second worst recession since the Great Depression. So I was unemployed, clueless about my future, and headed for divorce. I was a train wreck of a human being and hopelessly lost. I didn't know it then, but I was rapidly approaching rock bottom.

The great advantage of this yearlong catastrophe was that it served to make me painfully aware of just how screwed up I was. An uncommonly wise therapist to whom my wife and I had been going for marriage counseling, and who happened to be a pastor, graciously—but in no uncertain terms—pointed out to me the errors and hypocrisy of my behavior. Over the course of that year, it became evident to me how desperately I needed to change and how much I had to work on. It was overwhelming.

Though vital to my growth, these realizations were deeply agonizing and depressing. I felt tremendous regret for the mistakes I'd made, but I was also grieving the loss of what I thought was my entire future. I was heartbroken at the thought that I would never recover, never find the right girl, and never have a family. I wasn't just grieving the loss of the one relationship that I thought I might be able to trust (remember, trust didn't come easily for me); I was grieving what I thought was the loss of all hope, and that was devastating. The months after we split up were the hardest of my life. My despair was total. My fear was in full bloom.

Against this backdrop, about two months after my first wife left, very late on the night of November 9, 1983 (actually, in the early morning of November 10—ironically the exact date and very near the exact time of day when, six years later, I would experience the great high of my daughter being born), I was at my all-time low. I was twenty-six and experiencing the darkest moment of my life. After hours of a one-man pity party—the likes of which I have never come close to replicating—I found myself prostrate on the floor, sobbing, in tears, and begging (challenging) Jesus, if He really exists and if He really is God, for proof of His existence. I pleaded for help, guidance, and some assurance about my future. I got a response I hadn't expected.

A male voice spoke to me out of thin air. I still don't know if the voice was actually audible or if I just heard it in my head, but it was as clear as if someone were speaking to me face-to-face. An "Invisible Man" was in my living room! To this day I'm not 100 percent certain who spoke to me—He never identified Himself. What I do know is this: at the crescendo of my grief, I begged Jesus Christ for help, and I got a response in seconds. If it wasn't Jesus, it was somebody He sent.

I also know that I was not talking to myself. In fact, I wasn't talking at all. He was talking, and I was listening. This was not a conversation between peers. This Being carried a force of authority you would not think to disobey. He wasn't threatening in any way. He was more like a patient but powerful mentor who had just put His hand on my shoulder to calm me down and was now about to lead me through something that He knew I couldn't possibly understand. He had a weight and gravitas that by His very presence commanded respect.

Presence was an important aspect of this encounter: Someone *was* there. I could not see Him, but it was as if He were standing behind an invisible curtain speaking to me. I could hear His voice, and I could *feel* His presence in the room with me. It was unequivocally clear to me that whoever He was, He was superior to me—in fact, He was *vastly* superior—and I needed to listen to Him. Although He did nothing to provoke this response (other than speak), I felt overwhelmed and overpowered. I've had two medical emergencies in my life where I've physically gone into shock. This event was a lot like that, but this time my shock was emotional.

His opening words were "Write this down!" The statement was both an order and an assurance of a solution. It was spoken with total confidence, as if an expert were about to tell me, "Here's how we're going to fix this mess." The force and sensitivity of the statement were enough to make me stop crying. I got up, grabbed the first pen and piece of paper I saw, and started to write.

What came next was rapid-fire and cryptic, but very specific. A scan of my original notes appears on page 29.

The message had started coming before I could start writing, and I couldn't write as fast as the Invisible Man was speaking. Further complicating things was the fact that the first pen I grabbed was old, dry, and nearly out of ink. I had to run around the apartment looking for another pen while trying to take notes on the fly—a word or two to capture one idea and then on to the next point or back to get an earlier one that I had missed before I forgot it. I remember thinking that this felt like taking lecture notes in college. You can probably see in the scan where I changed pens at the start of the second-to-last line.

For those who can't read my writing and in order to clarify my shorthand, let me explain what I was told. This is from memory, so it may not be precisely verbatim. However, since the message was seared into my mind, what follows is pretty close to an exact quote, and the specific details of the prediction are in the actual sequence in which the message was delivered:

You will casually brush into your next, your "real,"
wife in mid-to-late September next year [1984].
The encounter will be very brief and completely
inconsequential. It will be nothing more than
enough to make the two of you aware of each

other. You will not actually meet her and truly get introduced until October 9, a few weeks later. [This date—October 9, 1984—was something He strongly emphasized.] *Physically, she will be a bit larger—both taller and more muscular—than your soon-to-be-ex-wife.* [He actually used my ex-wife's full first name, but I recorded it as her nickname; that is the rectangle blacked out in the scan of my notes.] *She will have brown hair and brown eyes. She will be right under your nose for months, but you will have no idea that she is the one. She will be aware of you that entire time as well. You'll be right under her nose, but she won't make any connection. And she will go by her middle name.*

Notice I originally counted only eight items on my notes. Initially, I counted coloring (hair and eyes) as one item and body type (height and musculature) as another. I separated the two pairs later because they were actually four individual traits. With my revised numbering, the message had ten components. There was a qualitative difference in the way the first nine items and the tenth and final item were conveyed. The first nine were communicated very precisely and meticulously. The last seemed to be almost casually included—as if He were throwing it in like an afterthought: "Oh yes, by the way, she will go by her middle name." I should also mention that I was not instructed to date my notes. After so many years in school, it was just force of habit.

11/10/83 ①   OCT. 9, 1984   ②   Deak Hein & Eyer shirt larger than ③

① She is a women & me as well. ⑤ W.J.I (trurhstoher in let Sept) i will

④ notice her but will not be interoduced until 10/9. he is want to see
(note)

⑦ She will be right under my nose, but ⟹ won't realize it
(me)

⑧ She will go by her middle name

My Original Notes

Although the entire encounter was strange, it was the first and last items on my list that really got to me. October 9, 1984 was a very specific date, and the idea that she would go by her middle name seemed so odd. But even aside from those details, the tone of the entire message was puzzling. This really wasn't a prediction, per se, or a command for me to do something; it was more a statement of fact. It was what I *would* do. A retelling of what would happen, because as I listened to Him speak, it was as if these events had already happened. It seemed more like a news report than a prediction.

And that was it. There were no good-byes. As fast as the conversation had started, it ended. It just stopped. The Invisible Man was gone. The whole episode probably didn't last more than a minute. It was the quintessential WTF moment. The experience has haunted me ever since, and I'm sure it will continue to haunt me for the rest of my life. The encounter was bizarre, totally outside of anything I had experienced. There was no way I could ignore it or forget about it. If God was trying to get my attention, He succeeded!

I begged for help, and He actually showed up! How do you deal with that? Had I been drinking, I think I would have assumed it was a hallucination. And I'm sure it would have scared me so badly that I would have sworn off alcohol forever. Unfortunately, I was dead sober, so I couldn't attribute this experience to one drink too many. At any rate, when the Invisible Man left, I was done crying. I sat there in a dazed state of shock.

I didn't know what to do. I didn't know what to

make of what had happened. I was intrigued by the possibility that what I had just experienced was real, but I certainly didn't trust that this was the case. I mean, really, if Jesus were willing to talk to me, why didn't He say something coherent? Is it possible that His preferred means of communication is to act like a guy who jumps into a cab, barks cryptic instructions to the driver, then immediately slides across the backseat, and gets out the other door, never to be seen again? This experience made no sense at all, and it genuinely made me fear for my sanity. Still, I hung onto my notes—just in case. And boy, am I glad I did!

I never dreamed I would guard that scrap of paper for the rest of my life. I never imagined how many times I would dig it out and stare at it to reassure myself that this event really happened. I never dreamed how often that note would give me hope or the courage to keep going. I also never dreamed I would share it one day.

I didn't realize it at the time, but I had just lived through the most important minute of my life. I also didn't realize that everything would be different after that.

In those first few minutes, I only grasped three things: First, there were the words of the message itself, which is what I focused on. Second, should the message prove true, I would have to confront the question, "How could this happen?" It was either a completely improbable, random fluke, or somebody was behind it. Third, whether the message proved true or false, there were implications either way.

If the message were false, I had experienced some form of psychotic event. Best case, this was simply an elaborate auditory hallucination. Worst case, I was exhibiting symptoms of schizophrenia. I was not only hearing voices, I was following their instructions. Not a comforting realization!

If, on the other hand, the message were true, I needed to consider the message behind the message—which was profound. I was vaguely aware of this fact immediately, but I didn't spend any time thinking about it. Truthfully, I tried to put it out of my mind.

The next morning I had to talk to somebody, so I confided in my mother and stepfather. I told them everything about what had happened. They didn't know what to think either, but neither suggested that I had gone over the deep end. My mother even circled October 9, 1984, on her calendar.

Later that day, I also called my best friend. He responded with all the reassurance and understanding that I'd come to expect from my college roommate and a guy I'd known since we were ten years old: "Yep, that settles it! You're crazy as hell!" Actually, that was just his initial response. We talked awhile longer, and he had a chance to absorb and reflect on the story I was telling him. He then came back with an interesting observation that could only have been made by someone who knew me as well as he did. He said, "You know, I don't think you were hallucinating." He paused for a moment, and then, with a laugh building in his voice, he added, "Because I've seen you when you were so stoned that you *were* hallucinating, and that's not how you hallucinate."

He made an interesting point, but the idea that some of the most debauched moments of my life could be used to authenticate the most sublime was ironic to say the least. It was also tragic. We both laughed at the absurdity of the logic, but even at twenty-six we knew our nervous laughter was covering a great deal of remorse. We ended the conversation agreeing that all I could do was to wait and see what happened. We hung up, and then life—as it always does—moved on.

CHAPTER THREE

And Now We Wait...

The thought of putting this event out of my mind never worked very well. So all I could do was wait and see whether: (a) God had actually intervened in my life, or (b) I was losing my mind.

A year had passed since my ex-wife had left. I had healed, continued to go to counseling, and started going to church. September 16, 1984, was a Sunday. I had a couple of friends over to my apartment that evening for a barbeque. I lived upstairs in the back of a four-unit apartment building. The entire street was comprised of the same four-unit apartment buildings, each one spaced about ten feet apart, each one the mirror image of the other.

A couple of weeks prior, a young couple had moved out of the apartment immediately across from mine in the upstairs unit next door. On September 15, the day before the barbeque, I had seen some people moving furniture into that vacant unit, but I had not met my new neighbors. That Sunday night, just after dark, there was a knock on my door while my friends and I were eating dinner by candlelight. I opened the door to a woman I didn't know.

She introduced herself as Claire. When she saw that we were in the middle of dinner, she apologized for the interruption. She quickly explained that she and her roommate had just moved in next door and their power wasn't on yet. When I realized who she was, I asked her if she'd like to come in. She declined. She told me she was a teacher and had early-morning playground duty the next day. She was wondering if I had a wind-up alarm clock that didn't require electricity. She had to be sure that she got to school on time and was afraid that, without an alarm, she might oversleep. I told her I didn't have a wind-up clock, but my wristwatch had an alarm. After testing the volume, she agreed the watch alarm would be fine, so I took it off, set the alarm for 5 AM, and handed it to her. She thanked me, apologized again for interrupting our dinner, and left. The encounter probably lasted two minutes. In the morning, I found that she had left my watch on my doorstep before I got up with a note that said, "Thanks." I thought nothing more about it.

I had started working at what was then one of the Big Eight accounting firms in January of 1984. Long hours have always been the norm in public accounting, and my experience with that firm was no exception. When I was on a client engagement, I typically got to work around eight in the morning and didn't get home till seven or eight at night. For the rest of September and early October, I was out at one of my big clients. This company was publicly traded and had some incredibly tight reporting deadlines, so quarter ends were always brutal. It wasn't uncommon for us to work twelve to sixteen hours a day, six or seven days a week, during these crunch periods. When the push was over, we could breathe, but nobody had a life while the heat was on. By the second week in October, we had met the reporting deadline, and I was able to get a little break.

October 9 of that year was a Tuesday. I got home about 5:30 that afternoon. I was more than a little distraught. The day was, for all intents and purposes, gone. I had been mindful of the date since waking up that morning. I'd known I would be at client sites all day. If I were going to meet anyone, I assumed, it would happen while I was out and about. I'd had hope while I was out in public, but now that I was home, where I lived alone, I had no chance of meeting anyone. The day had come and gone. I'd met no one. Nothing. Not so much as a hint of opportunity. So much for God and His promises!

As I climbed the stairs to my apartment, I was moving toward another pity party. Home alone now, I felt like all chances of meeting someone were lost. When I walked in, I completely closed the door on any hope that my encounter with God had been real. I cursed myself for my stupidity, for having placed even the slightest bit of faith in that idiotic brain-fart of almost a year ago. *What could I have been thinking? What was wrong with me that I would dare think God would bother with me?* I knew I couldn't just sit there and descend further into the abyss. I had to get out and clear my head. Somehow life would go on. I fought off my growing depression and changed clothes to go for a run.

At about six o'clock, I opened my door to step out for my run. As I turned back to lock the door, I heard the door of the upstairs apartment immediately across from me open and close. I didn't know it then, but that was the door to hope reopening. As I turned again to walk across my porch to the top of my stairs, I found myself looking directly across at the girl who had come over nearly a month before to borrow the alarm clock. I had been so busy with work that I hadn't seen her since. We couldn't miss seeing each other now, though: we were walking straight toward each other, just thirty feet apart. We hit the top of our stairs at exactly the same time and started down in lockstep. She was wearing running clothes as well.

I'm not positive who spoke first, but I think she said something like "I haven't seen you around." I said I'd been working a lot. And it turned out she was gone most weekends, visiting her boyfriend who lived ninety miles away. These circumstances didn't facilitate our casually running into each other. It also reinforced for me right off the bat that she was not available. Being down already, I didn't need to get hit over the head to get that message. Trying to be cordial, I observed that it looked like she was going for a run too. She said she hadn't gone on a run since she moved in and didn't have a route in mind. She asked where she should go if she wanted to do about four miles. I told her that my short route was about five miles and that was my plan that night. I asked if she just wanted to follow me. She said sure, as long as we took it slowly.

We started running, and we talked as we ran. We went at a slower pace than I was used to, so the run took longer than usual. When we got back home, we walked around the block to cool down. After that, we sat at the bottom of my stairs and talked for close to another hour until it got very dark and we started to get cold. As we headed up our separate but parallel staircases to our respective apartments, I remember thinking that she seemed very nice. I also couldn't help but note that (just like the Invisible Man's prediction) she had brown hair and brown eyes. And, at nearly 5'8," she was about an inch and a half taller and much more athletic than the slight actress who was by then my ex-wife. Unfortunately, all that said, she also had a long-term boyfriend to whom she was practically engaged. That pretty much killed all possibilities. There was clearly no reason for me to be excited. We said goodnight as we each walked across our porches to our own front door.

We ran three or four more times over the next two weeks. I was getting home early enough that our schedules were aligning. Our coming out of our front doors at exactly the same time happened often enough that it was starting to become a bit of a joke.

Claire and I were developing a casual friendship when our evening runs got interrupted. It was late October, and I started having some stomach issues— an intense pain on my lower right side. This came and went for a while until one day in early November when it didn't go away. I went home from work early, thinking I had the flu. The pain built throughout the evening and into the night. I started thinking I might have appendicitis, but some of the symptoms were missing. When the fever and vomiting kicked in around 4:30 AM and I started to double over in pain, I finally decided I better get to the hospital.

By the time I arrived at the emergency room and saw a doctor, my appendix was about to burst. The surgeons got it out before it ruptured, but this was almost thirty years ago, back when they made a real four-to-five-inch incision for appendectomies. They also had to irrigate my gut to be sure nothing had leaked. I remember waking up thinking, *So this is what it feels like to be stabbed*. After I spent a couple of nights in the hospital, they let me go home, but I was still pretty weak. I couldn't drive, and the surgeon didn't want me climbing stairs, so I spent a night or two at my parents' place before I insisted on going back to my own apartment.

I was stuck at home, unable to even go downstairs to get my mail for a couple of days. On the third day I finally went down to my mailbox about 4 PM. I was making my way back upstairs—pasty white, one slow step at a time—when Claire got home from school and saw me on the stairs. One look and she knew something was wrong. (Other than having lost fifteen pounds, being white as a sheet, and sweating profusely, I'm not sure what gave me away.) I explained what had happened, and she dropped her stuff and helped me upstairs. All the while that I was telling her "I'm fine," I was secretly grateful she had shown up. I wasn't sure I could have made it back to my apartment alone. After she got me settled on the couch, Claire ran home, changed, and then went to the market for me. *Rather decent of her*, I thought.

That was the real start of our friendship. Claire would come over and we would just talk—for hours. When I was home early enough, and once I was better, we would run together in the evening. If she were around on the weekend, we would talk during the day, and then I would go out on dates at night. The fact that she was involved with someone else, and I was dating as much as I could, actually freed us up to get to know each other without any expectations. I just assumed there was no possibility of a relationship with her, so I never connected the dots the Invisible Man had outlined for me.

Things were purely platonic until about the end of the next summer. That's when Claire started calling her boyfriend by my name, and I started to realize that I had a much better time talking with Claire than I did with any of the girls I had been dating.

By the end of Labor Day weekend in '85, I realized I had feelings for Claire and told her I loved her. She broke up with her boyfriend, and we started dating immediately thereafter. About a month or so later—and almost two years after my encounter with the Invisible Man—I was over at Claire's apartment and saw some mail on the kitchen counter. One envelope was an electric bill addressed to Marie Claire Benton. "What's this?" I asked. I thought it must be a mistake. She explained that her mother had named her after her best friend from college, Marie, but she had always gone by Claire.

By this point Claire and I had talked for hundreds of hours. I had met her friends and family. I had seen her mail on multiple occasions. No one, anywhere, *ever*, called her Marie! I'd known guys who went by their middle name, but I'd never known or even heard of any woman going by her middle name. (I've done a little research since then, and it's estimated that only one to two percent of women in the US go by their middle name.) Now, nearly thirty years later, I still do not personally know another woman who goes by her middle name! Given all this, when I found out that *Claire* was actually Claire's middle name, I was shocked.

Right up until that moment, I would have said that everything that had happened—even though the events had happened just as predicted—was nothing more than coincidence. If for no other reason than self-protection, I couldn't let myself accept the possibility that reality was unfolding as the Invisible Man had said it would. While I sure hoped that what I had experienced was real, I have to admit that I had no faith that was the case. I was too afraid of being hurt to trust a voice that I might have invented. Plus, right up until that moment, I was also sure that the last bit of the message—about her going by her middle name—was wrong. As far as I was concerned, if part of the message was wrong, all of it was wrong, and then none of it could have been a message from God, because God doesn't make mistakes!

After Claire told me about her name, everything changed. I could no longer pretend that the prediction of two years earlier was just a coincidence. I could no longer ignore that something remarkable had happened; I had to take it seriously. We were engaged by Christmas and married in August '86. I was head over heels in love. I'd never felt that way before— further reinforcing what a mistake my first marriage had been.

In the years since Claire and I married, we've certainly had our struggles. There have been times when I've asked God, "Why did You do this to me?" I know she's done the same. All that said, she remains the most honest, decent, innately kind, and devoted person I've ever met. She's a brilliant mother, educator, and coach for other parents. We've raised two kids who are the greatest joys of my life. And we're still together nearly thirty years later.

Had Claire not shown up, I never would have become the father, husband, or man that I am today. My life would have been hopelessly incomplete without her.

CHAPTER FOUR

What Just Happened?

N one of the details of the prediction had unfolded as I had imagined they might, but all ten of the points I had written down two years earlier had come to pass just as the Invisible Man said they would. It's one thing to accurately predict ten out of ten details about dates, physical description, proximity, and name from a known set of variables. The odds that such a prediction could happen by chance are roughly five billion to one. It's quite another thing to accurately select ten specific variables from a population of all possible variables and then to accurately predict the precise sequence in which those selected variables would be realized over the next two years. The odds that the prediction I recorded could happen by chance are unfathomably small.

Wrapping my head around this extraordinary sequence of events was a two-step process. The first step involved reaching a conclusion about what had actually happened; the second involved processing what it all meant. I got closure on the first step within days of learning that Claire went by her middle name; I've spent decades on the second. While I still don't have it completely figured out, I've gradually realized some things that have profoundly changed my life. I'll explain the first step now and the second in a minute.

As for what actually happened, I think there are three possible explanations: First, I randomly dreamed up a prediction and it randomly came true. Second, I experienced some kind of auditory hallucination, and over the course of the next two years, I subconsciously manipulated my life—and the life of a woman I had never met—to orchestrate the fulfillment of all ten criteria that were predicted during that hallucination. Third, in the midst of my grief, God Himself took pity on me, decided to intervene, and shared with me elements of the soon-to-be story of my life.

Let's take these three options one at a time. The idea that this was a completely random event is, in my opinion, absurd. I can't buy it for two reasons. First, the nature and context of the message stand alone in my experience: I have never encountered anything comparable. Second, the idea that the generation and fulfillment of this prediction could be random strains even my capacity for self-delusion. I've had enough statistical training to know that the odds that this could have happened by chance are virtually impossible. In fact, to say that the fulfillment of this prediction was statistically improbable is an understatement comparable to saying that it is unlikely a man could stand on the surface of the earth and jump to the surface of the moon.

I can't buy the second option either. In the last several years, a number of theories have been floated about near-death experiences and angelic encounters. Some of these theories suggest that, in times of extreme duress, our brains engage some form of primal survival mechanism that tricks us into believing we are being assisted by a divine power. No doubt some people will offer this as an explanation for what I experienced, but I think there is a big problem with this theory. My Invisible Man specifically predicted ten criteria in the exact sequence in which I would realize them over the next two years. Unless our brains have the ability to travel through time and report back on future events, I don't think this theory works.

Although it is still hard for me to accept the third option without question, I see no real alternative. I don't believe in God because I'm a man of great faith. I believe in God because I was confronted with a firsthand experience that I can't dismiss. I've done the math! I believe because I no longer have the option of *not* believing. When somebody hits me over the head, I tend to take that person seriously. You're welcome to disagree with the conclusions I draw below about who God is and how He wants us to behave. I readily admit that, over the last thirty years, I have often had my doubts and have regularly challenged these conclusions myself; however, I have always returned to the same conclusions. All that said, given my experience, there is one conclusion I have never challenged: God *is* real, and we *are not* alone.

Unfortunately, He didn't give me any way to prove His existence to anyone else. I wrote my notes on the night it happened, I kept them all these years, and I scanned them to include in this book. I could have faked all of that. I didn't, but of course I can't prove that. I told three people of my encounter within hours of it happening, and I told a fourth two years later. I could have lied to them. Again, I didn't, but I can't prove that either.

Only I know what really happened: I begged Jesus Christ for help, and either He—or somebody He sent—showed up and helped me. In less than a minute, He proved to me He was real, He modeled for me how He treats people, and, by so doing, I believe He also modeled for me how He wants me to treat other people. In essence, He gave me an object lesson. Once I accepted the reality of God's existence, I realized I had to follow His example.

It took me awhile to get a handle on God's object lesson and to begin to reach some conclusions about what this experience meant. After years of reflection, I've come to believe that He was trying to tell me ten things:

1. "There is a God. I am He. I'm here, and I'm real."

I'm convinced I encountered a Being who either is or who works for the Creator of the universe. The fact that He knows who I am is both sobering and mind-boggling.

2. *"I'm paying attention."*

God had been watching me the entire time I was completely ignoring Him. He waited to intervene until I hit rock bottom and called out to Him for help. His timing was perfect.

3. *"I care."*

He didn't have to intervene. I wouldn't have known the difference had He never lifted a finger. He had the perfect out, but He didn't take it. He chose to help me.

4. *"I'm approachable."*

God Almighty never even hinted at His infinite power. He never postured or positioned. He didn't impose Himself on me in any way. He could not have been more gracious.

5. *"I give and forgive unconditionally."*

He helped me without requiring me to meet any preconditions. He didn't demand anything in advance or in return. He didn't reprimand me or criticize me for getting myself into this mess. There was no "I told you so" or "I'll help you if you do _____." There was no punishment or threat of consequences if I didn't shape up. All the condemnation I deserved, I never got. He didn't even ask for an apology. All I got was kindness and reassurance. I had given Him no incentive to treat me with anything other than contempt, but He chose instead to graciously offer assistance.

6. "I take the long view."

He has a much bigger perspective on events than I do. He obviously sees things that I don't. He is willing to act on His broader perspective and stay the course to achieve a greater good even if His actions frustrate me.

7. "I know you like a father knows his child."

He knew how to get my attention. He knew what to say to snap me out of my downward spiral. He knew how to capture my imagination and give me hope. He knew how to overwhelm me with evidence that I couldn't ignore. He knew how to convince me. He knew how to send messages within a message that I could understand. You really have to know your audience to do that—and to do it in seconds is incredible.

I couldn't grasp this parent/child analogy until I became a father, but my first child taught me that it's possible to know exactly what your child needs before he does. By the time our son was a toddler, Claire and I could predict what he was going to do next. I've talked to many parents who have experienced the same thing. It took me years to realize that God had done the same thing with me.

8. *"I want you to grow."*

God gave me just enough information to get me to suspend my disbelief and to hold open the possibility that what I had experienced might be real. He didn't give me answers; He gave me the promise of answers. He's much more concerned with my growth than my comfort. He wants me to struggle with things and figure them out for myself. He's willing to give me the time and space to do that because He knows that if He bails me out, I won't learn anything. He's never handed me the answers to life on a silver platter, but He's given me a new life.

9. *"I'm trustworthy."*

At the highest level, His unspoken message to me was "Trust Me." The basic theme I've heard from Him in the thirty years since this intervention has been "I'm going to take you on a journey. You're going to discover things along the way. Both the journey itself and the things you discover are going to change you and cause you to grow. But you're going to have to trust Me and follow Me to get where you want to go, because I'm not going to carry you."

He made me wait and watch and learn how things would come together. This was very hard for me because, as I've mentioned, at that time I found it nearly impossible to trust anybody. There were plenty of dark nights during those ensuing two years, but the results were worth it. He came through. There have been many more dark nights during the ensuing thirty years as well, but in the end He has always come through. I hate to admit how easy it still is for me to forget that fact when I get scared. I often have to remind myself that He's never failed me yet.

10. *"I'm more playful than you think."*

God was accurate without being specific. He described exactly what would happen without giving away the end of the story. He knew I would eventually figure it out, but He wanted me to learn something through the process. I think He likes riddles, and I bet He delivered the message with a grin on His face. I think He was playing with me in the same way a parent plays Hide and Seek with an infant. He was trying to teach me that just because you can't see something, doesn't mean it's not there!

If I put together all the traits He modeled (being present, compassionate, humble, forgiving, gracious, kind, patient, committed, faithful, intimate, encouraging, assisting, teaching, trustworthy, playful), I think I have an illustration of how to give love. If I consider the state I was in when God intervened in my life, I think I have an illustration of how much love I need to give.

I have to remember that His answer to my prayer was nothing I deserved or was entitled to. In fact, I had done everything in my power to prove I didn't deserve it. I wasn't some innocent victim. I had brought the disaster upon myself. He stepped in and helped me in spite of what I had done. He knew what I was, He knew what He was getting into, and He showed up anyway. He didn't hold my past against me. He didn't condemn me even though He had every right to do so. What He did instead was show me love, grace, compassion, and hope.

This is the Christianity I know. This is the God I try to follow. This is the posture of the heart and humility of spirit I try to emulate. If He could show me unconditional love, I think I have to do the same with everybody else—*regardless* of what they are, do, have done, or believe. If He didn't judge or condemn me, when I was at my worst, I don't see how I can judge or condemn anybody else. When Jesus famously said, "I am the way," this is the "way" I think He was talking about. When I said earlier that all that follows in this book is based on this premise and worldview, this is the base of which I speak.

Now, being aware of these principles, have I successfully and consistently put them into practice? Absolutely not! I still have a very, very long way to go. But this is a checklist I try to remind myself of daily.

CHAPTER FIVE

An Education in Life and Death

Our first year of marriage was rough. From the time we got home from our honeymoon in early September until the first of March, I worked between ninety and a hundred hours a week. In early December we found out Claire was pregnant. By Christmas she had horrible morning sickness, and it lasted the entire pregnancy. And I was no help to her at all.

At a time when I most needed to support my wife, I was both physically and emotionally unavailable. I was buried by work and hated my job, but I felt I had to keep going. I had a child coming, and I had to provide for that child. The memory of the fear of losing my home at seventeen had not gone away. I never wanted my kids to know that fear. So making money was suddenly all that mattered to me, and I was ignoring the very gift I had begged God for three years before.

From the beginning of March until mid-June of '87, I was on the road nonstop. I would fly out

Monday morning and fly home Friday night. By late June, with the baby due in two months, I had to make a decision—my job or my family. I'd gotten what I needed out of the accounting firm, and they'd taken their pound of flesh out of me. Leaving was an easy decision. However, the uncertainty of being unemployed eight weeks before the baby's due date was tough.

As it turned out, I had little to worry about. I joined a start-up company one week before our son was born. I was now working only a few miles from home, the hours were half what I was used to, and the pay was double. All in all, things were much easier—but the difficulties from our first year lingered. Neither of us was emotionally equipped to deal with and resolve the tremendous strain we had experienced. In spite of the growth I'd achieved in the previous few years, I still had a very long way to go. Fortunately, Claire and I had two things holding us together: a newborn and a shared commitment to a faith that was bigger than ourselves. Without those two things, I wonder whether our marriage would have survived.

Babies are incredible. I loved my son to death, but he brought a lot of change and exhaustion to our marriage. Two years later, we had another baby, a little girl. I don't think it would be possible for us to be more fortunate with our kids. I am truly the luckiest dad in the world. My son and my daughter brought me joy that I had lost as a child and that I didn't think I could ever find again. I did nothing to earn or create that joy.

It was a gift. The greatest regret of my life is that I was so stressed during the two pregnancies, worried about how I would provide for these children, when I should have been euphoric with excitement over what an incredible blessing they would be. Another lesson learned.

By the time our daughter was born in late '89, I was once again working crazy hours to get my employer ready for an initial public offering. Even when my ninety-year-old grandmother had a major stroke two months after the birth, I was trapped at work. I got the call at 10 AM that she was in the hospital and likely wouldn't make it, but because I was working on documents for the offering registration—that had to be drafted and delivered to our corporate counsel by that evening—I didn't make it to the hospital until 9 PM. I got to her bedside only a couple of hours before she died.

After the company's public offering, my workload increased again. Then, in September and against my wishes, Claire reduced her work hours to part-time so she could spend more time with the kids. I couldn't see this move as a good thing; all I could see was that it put more financial pressure on me. I am now ashamed to admit how self-centered I was then and how little importance I attached to a mother being more engaged with her children. At the time, all I could think about was building financial stability for our family and getting a real house for our kids. I failed to appreciate that Claire and the kids couldn't have cared less about all that. I really wasn't working for them; I was working for me. I was trying to prove that I was a good provider. I know

I'm not the only guy who has made these mistakes, but that doesn't make them any easier to admit.

The opportunity with the start-up appeared to have run its course, and the telltale signs of trouble soon appeared on the horizon. I'd had reservations about my boss, the CFO, ever since my first interview when he made a statement I'll never forget: "I never become friends with the people who work for me in case I have to f**k them over." That line spoke volumes, but I didn't attach the weight to it that it deserved. I should have.

As the company's revenue and earnings growth started to slow, the CEO and CFO sought increasingly "creative" ways to meet Wall Street's expectations. When I refused to go along with a move that I regarded as outright fraud, the CFO went around me and promoted one of my ethically challenged subordinates who was so eager to advance that he willingly agreed to do what I refused to do—even though he knew full well it was wrong. When the house of cards came down, the stock collapsed, investors sued, and the SEC investigated. The CFO blamed the entire mess on my former subordinate whom he had promoted around me and then very publicly fired him. I felt sorry for the guy, but I had warned him: you sleep with the devil and these things happen. It had been very difficult to take an ethical stand against my boss and the CEO. I'd paid a high price because of it (my career at that company was effectively ended), but the price would have been much higher had I gone along with what I knew to be wrong.

Fortunately, by the time the company imploded, I had already left to join a small consulting practice. I stayed with that practice for three years, but did nine years' worth of work and became a road warrior during that time. I hit all but a handful of states and regularly woke up in hotels wondering where I was. The time was exhausting but productive: my partners and I used our client engagements as an opportunity to build a new software application. By early '95, it looked like we could turn it into a real company, so we went out to raise some capital.

As I was entering a new phase of my life, a part of my old life was coming to an end. After my father left in '74, my brother and I had become very close to my dad's younger brother, and then, a few years later, to our stepfather as well. These guys were both serial entrepreneurs, and they had given me the bug. They had both had hits and misses over the years, but on balance had done okay. My uncle never married and had no children. My stepfather had been previously married, but had gone through a rough divorce and was subsequently estranged from his kids. So at a time when my brother and I were looking for father figures, my uncle and stepfather were, in their own ways, looking for sons. I suspect we all filled voids in each other's lives, and I know they made a big difference in mine.

In the spring of '95, doctors determined that my uncle needed a second heart bypass. Within days of the news, my stepfather was diagnosed with cancer. They both went into surgery at the same hospital at 9 AM on the same day. My stepfather's cancer had metastasized and was found to be extremely aggressive, but he still did better than my uncle.

My uncle was severely diabetic. He ended up being on the operating table for twelve hours for what should have been a five-hour surgery. He never healed properly. His chest literally split open three weeks following his operation. Over the next seven months, he spent only three days out of the hospital. He had several emergency surgeries, spent months in the ICU, and almost died several times before he finally did. The ordeal was agony for him and gut-wrenching for my brother and me. We were at his bedside almost every day. By the time he died, we had held all-night vigils and watched the sunrise from the hospital more times than I can count. Meanwhile, my stepfather started chemo and radiation. I barely saw my wife and kids during those months.

I had recently succeeded in funding my own start-up, and we had just moved into our first house when my brother called at 2 AM one night to tell me our uncle was dead. As we cleaned out his house and I worked on the start-up, I sank into a depression that lasted about four months. I did my best to hide it and continued to work. Then my mother was diagnosed with cancer. More surgery, more chemo, more radiation. She recovered; my stepfather relapsed. More surgery, more chemo, more radiation. By December of '98 we all knew that this Christmas would probably be his last.

I've found that when someone you love dies a long, debilitating death, it's like a piece of them is stolen each day. Then, one day, there's simply nothing left. It's horrible for the patient, but in many ways it's as hard on their family members who are forced to live from crisis to crisis, helplessly riding the emotional roller coaster from despair to hope and back again.

This process destroyed my illusion of invincibility. For the first time I "owned" my mortality. The realization dawned on me that such trials can befall anyone and that it's only by the grace of God that they don't.

During the time that all of this was going on, I was trying to build a company, travelling constantly, trying to support my parents, and trying to be a husband and father. And that was the order of my priorities. My focus on the business and the health of my parents was much greater than my focus on my wife and kids. At home I was on autopilot.

By January '99, Claire and I were at loggerheads, and she was nearing the end of her rope. She left me a short note right after New Year's that rocked me more than she knew. I've hung onto it as a reminder:

> *This is a desperate plea to try to save our marriage. I feel I am withering away from loneliness, lack of intimacy and general interest from you. I am past the point of being hurt because I know you don't act so disengaged out of meanness. Your involvement in your dream / business is stunning to me for I've not lived with this kind of obsession*

until I married. I need more balance. I feel I'm losing strength and stamina. I am lost. I don't know what to do.

I obviously had a major problem. I also had a long way to go to become a decent husband and father. These were goals I professed to want badly, but I had not invested in, or committed to, making those goals a reality.

Claire's note ripped me apart. Her plea deeply affected me, but I never let on how much. She wanted action at this point, not words. I privately grieved over the pain I'd caused. I knew I had to change, but I didn't really understand the ways in which I needed to change.

Seven months later something happened that finally made it clear to me.

CHAPTER SIX

I Don't Think Hell Is What I Thought It Was

I n late March of '99, I got a call that my father needed an emergency bypass. He was scheduled for surgery the next day. My brother and I reluctantly grabbed a flight. All I could think about on the airplane was *Here we go again*.

My father was movie-star handsome, an athlete, a Korean War veteran, highly educated, and an accomplished professional. He spent his entire career as an educator devoting himself to the needs of severely mentally and physically handicapped children. He went out of his way to care for kids with horrific challenges, and he was always gentle, compassionate, and kind to children whom many in society would prefer to sweep under the rug. Unfortunately, as I explained earlier, he also had an addiction that ruined his life and harmed a lot of other people as well.

As a kid I had idolized my dad. I kissed him good-bye each morning before school and good night each evening he was home. After he left, all that changed. Over the ensuing twenty-five years, until his death, I saw him maybe a dozen times and talked to him no more than thirty. Each conversation became more disheartening than the last as he boasted of both past experiences and more recent, increasingly perverse escapades with his new wife, who shared his enthusiasm for "the lifestyle."

Once unencumbered by any pretense of family restraints, my father indulged his habit fully and often. He wasn't ashamed or embarrassed; nor was he regretful. To the contrary, he told me point-blank that in spite of the damage done to his family, career, and other relationships, he was glad to have had his many sexual experiences.

Toward the end, the only people close to my father were those who shared his passion for sex and wealth. He became alienated and estranged from his family, friends, and professional colleagues—anyone who had been close to him when he was a younger man. He was consumed by his addiction in the same way an unrecovered alcoholic is ultimately consumed by booze.

In the last years of his life, the only two topics my father would talk about were sex and money. Any attempt to change the topic was met with silence and then a quick segue back to one of those two themes. If troublesome issues of life crept into the conversation, he would jump back to a discussion of sex or money, much like a junkie getting his fix to forestall the agony of withdrawal. When he did this, his entire physical and emotional countenance changed from great anxiety to euphoric relief as his own special narcotic temporarily blocked the pain of the real world. It came as no surprise that these were the last topics on his lips as the surgical team wheeled him into the operating room for his heart bypass.

The operation did not go well. Emergency surgery in the middle of the night was required to repair a leaking bypass that nearly killed him. He spent the next two months in the hospital, slowly recovering, before he was finally deemed well enough to go home.

He called me just after he got home. He was tired, but hugely relieved to be out of the hospital. He also had some other good news. In the run-up of the Internet bubble, a stock he owned had risen dramatically and closed that day at an all-time high. He had finally realized a dream he had longed for his entire life: he had officially become a millionaire. He was very happy, but too tired to talk long. Our call was short. It would be our last.

He lived in the South, and I in the West. As I said, my brother and I had gone down for the surgery, but only stayed a couple of days, just until it looked like he was out of the woods. I had a business to run, and within weeks I would have another crisis on my hands.

Claire discovered a lump in her right breast. Mammograms confirmed the mass. A review of the prior year's mammogram proved more unsettling. The radiologist had spotted the same suspicious mass a year ago and flagged it for immediate follow-up, but an internal mix-up had occurred. The radiologist's staff had forwarded the wrong patient's report—which said that everything was fine—to Claire's physician. I actually discovered the mistake when reviewing her entire medical record as we transported the files to the surgeon. The mass was now five times larger than it had been a year earlier.

The surgeon tried a needle biopsy with little success. The mass was as hard as a rock, and the edges were not particularly clean. Not good signs. The odds were growing that this was cancer. They scheduled Claire for surgery in two days, and we started the prep—blood work, pre-surgical exams, insurance pre-authorization, etc.

Late that afternoon—after the attempted biopsy—was when my father had gone home from the hospital and called to tell me he was rich. That night, however, he was the last person I was thinking about. My wife was scared to death, I was too, and we were trying not to worry the kids. Neither of us got much sleep that night.

The next morning, one day before Claire's surgery, we were up early, as usual, getting the kids off to school. I was taking a couple of days off work to attend to the last pre-op appointments and to be there with her at the hospital. Suddenly, around 7:30 AM, I started having the strangest, most overwhelming feelings of remorse and regret I've ever experienced. It was the kind of remorse you feel as a parent when you really screw up with your kids and realize it afterward—but this remorse had nothing to do with either my kids or Claire's upcoming surgery.

This feeling was shocking because of the

overwhelming intensity of the emotion. I had a secondary awareness that there was no way back, no hope of recourse or reconciliation. And, strangest of all, I could tell that the feelings weren't coming from me. I knew somehow that they were coming from my father. It was as if I were feeling what *he* was feeling.

His grief was inconsolable; his despair, total. He had suddenly realized that he had made a catastrophic error, but he had no way to make it right. He had walked away from the people who loved him most, and there was no second chance. No hope of redemption or reprieve. No way to fix what he had broken. No one to assuage his pain or comfort him over his loss. He bore the weight of this anguish alone. That weight was crushing and could not be lifted—*ever*. He had to live, forever, with what he had done. The book was closed. The door was shut.

This sense was so powerful it was crippling. It was also intimate. It was as if he were right next to me, but again hidden by a curtain. I could *feel* his presence. I could almost hear him sobbing. I just couldn't see him. I sat down with my head in my hands and could hardly speak. The depression was incredible. I have never experienced anything like this grief before or since.

Claire couldn't help but notice that something was wrong, and she asked if I was okay. I tried to explain what I was feeling and that it was about my father, but it didn't make any more sense to her than it did to me. The emotions were so out of context that it never occurred to me that anything was actually wrong with him. As far as I knew, he was fine.

At about 8:30 AM, the phone rang. My father had died on the couch about an hour before. His wife was calling from the hospital parking lot. She had accompanied the paramedics to the emergency room as they tried to revive him. Their efforts hadn't worked, and she had spent some time with his cardiologist afterward trying to figure out what had happened before she called me. She and the cardiologist were shocked. Both of them had expected him to make a full recovery.

The emotions I was experiencing grew throughout the day, but began to abate the next, the day of Claire's surgery. By the time she was out of recovery and the surgeon gave us the all clear, the feelings from my father had all but disappeared. The memory of these emotions, however, has never gone away.

It's been fourteen years since my father died. I don't know for certain what was actually happening, or exactly what I was sensing, during the thirty-six-hour period from the morning he died until the afternoon of the next day, but I certainly have a theory. I believe my father was sending me a message: an apology for what he now regretted and a warning about how I needed to change.

That message caused me to also believe that if there is an actual, physical place called Hell, it's not a place where someone persecutes or torments you. It's a place where you are allowed to persecute and torment yourself. It's a place where you are presented with your missed opportunities, made fully aware of the better alternatives you opted not to pursue, and given all the uninterrupted time in the universe to reflect on the love you lost. It's a place where you are allowed to fully appreciate the path you chose in juxtaposition to the path you chose to ignore. It's a place where God, being the consummate gentleman that He is, sadly but respectfully acknowledges your decisions and provides you with a quiet spot to live with your choices—forever.

Whatever it was that I experienced, it turned out to be one of the greatest gifts of my life. I would like to think that my father's message—like that of Jacob Marley's ghost visiting Ebenezer Scrooge—saved me from repeating his fate. And by so doing, he also taught me a great deal about forgiveness: nothing I could do would punish him as much as he was now punishing himself.

Whatever lingering anger or resentment I held toward my father was gone. All I felt now was sympathy for his loss, compassion for his pain, and the chilling realization that while I hadn't made his mistakes, I'd made plenty of others. That realization led directly to another: I didn't ever want to experience the kind of regret about my life that my father was now experiencing about his. The thought of it scared me to death!

Until the day my father died, I was actively engaged in the cultivation of my own addiction: I was a workaholic. I professed to want financial security for my family, but it was more than that. I wanted wealth, status, prestige, etc., in order to prove my worth and dispel my sense of inadequacy—probably exactly the same mind-set that drove my father to fill his void by bedding every woman he could get and buying the most expensive cars he could afford.

Although I would have vehemently denied it at the time (and I would have been convinced that I was telling the truth), the reality is that I was putting wealth, power, and image ahead of the people in my life. I was very materialistic and image conscious, and I was completely missing the most beautiful gifts of life that were right in front of me. I couldn't miss the irony of the fact that my father died within hours of getting the money he'd coveted for a lifetime. I also couldn't forget that I had been threatened with the prospect of losing my wife. I had to change!

CHAPTER SEVEN

Heaven Isn't What I Thought It Was Either

Four months after my father died, I was alone with my stepfather when he died. The day after his funeral, we were back in the hospital with my mother, who was going into surgery to have another tumor removed. Thankfully, this one was benign, so the follow-up was easy. But only after we found out that she was okay was I able to let down my guard. When I did, I sank into another major depression.

I forced myself to keep going through the motions of life, but life was going on around me, not with me. In January 2000, at a time when I could barely function, I made over $2 million on a penny stock I'd held for several years. Within three weeks I closed on a major round of capital for my own business. My stake in my company was now worth $9 million. I was worth $11 million—on paper, at least. (That turned out to be an important caveat....) I should have been euphoric. Instead, I was numb.

I had been working my tail off for twenty-five years. I had bounced from one health crisis to the next for the last five years. I had watched each of the three men I was closest to die a long, debilitating death. I had thought at different times that I might also lose my wife and my mother. Now, after so many business struggles and disappointments, everything seemed to just fall into place.

Old friends told me I was "done," that I had "arrived," but there was emptiness in that arrival. The guys I most wanted to celebrate this victory with were gone. The lesson of my father's death was reinforced. No amount of money could buy back what I'd lost.

Money wasn't making me happy. So I bought a forty-one-foot yacht. Surely *that* would cheer me up. I'd wanted one for years, and this would be my reward for all my hard work. I planned to chill out on the boat, to relax a bit as I waited to sell the business and cash in the rest of my equity. What a joke! Owning a boat was a bigger headache than owning a business. I'd never realized how much work or stress was involved—or that B.O.A.T. really stands for "Break Out Another Thousand!"

Meanwhile, our investors had insisted on bringing in a new chief executive from IBM to rapidly grow our sales. His plan never seemed like a good idea to my partner and me. We begged the board not to follow him and carefully laid out our case for all the things we thought could go wrong. They didn't agree with us. We weren't sales guys, so what did we know? The board gave the CEO the green light, and things promptly proceeded to go even worse than my partner and I had feared that they might.

First, Y2K came and went. Software spending went way down. Next, the Internet bubble burst. Stock prices collapsed, and so did investment in early-stage tech companies. The final straw was 9/11.

We were never a "dot-gone." We had a real, nationally recognized, award-winning product. We had customers who loved us. We had great analyst reviews. We had revenues in the millions. We just ran out of cash, and the only investors we could find who still had cash wanted terms that were so outrageous that our board wouldn't accept them. In early '03, we closed on the sale of our business to a much larger public company. Timing is everything. We sold it for a fraction of what it had been worth when we were in negotiations to sell to a Fortune 500 the year before.

I had counted my chickens before they hatched. Fortunately, other than purchasing the boat, I'd been financially conservative, but I was still left with only one-sixth of what I had been worth on paper three years earlier.

Speaking of the boat… After consuming tens of thousands of dollars, it had one more thing to take from me: my spine. On July 4, 2002, I was lifting a dinghy out of the water and onto the back swim step when a sudden four-foot wave kicked up the stern of the boat like it was a forty-one-foot teeter-totter. Between the 200-pound dinghy pulling me down and the deck raising me up, I ruptured two discs in my lower back. I got rid of the boat shortly before we sold the company.

As a condition of the acquisition, I was contractually

required to stay on as an employee of the company that bought us for one year. The pain in my back grew worse as scars formed over the ruptures on the discs. My pain over the acquisition grew the more I traveled and the more unethical I realized our new employer was. I left fifteen minutes after I cashed my last golden handcuff check.

A few months after the acquisition, in the summer of '03, I went on a two-week, eighty-mile backpacking trip in the Southern Rockies with my son and some friends. I had to get my spine shot full of cortisone and live on Advil in order to make the hike, but I wouldn't have missed it for the world. It was the most wonderful trip of my life—as close to Heaven as I've ever been.

Halfway through that trip, on the anniversary of the day my father had left twenty-nine years before, I finally got it. Yachts didn't do it. Cars didn't do it. Having a million dollars in the bank didn't make me happy or bring me peace and joy. Being free, in the middle of nowhere with nothing more than a backpack, tent, and sleeping bag, surrounded by people I cared about, did. Once I realized that and once I realized the date, all I could do was laugh at my own stupidity, shake my head at the irony of it all, and wonder why it took me so damn long to figure things out. Thank God I finally did!

On that day, I became a student of my faith, my family, my life, and myself—and I haven't looked back since. I've tried to invest daily in becoming the type of person I want to be. I've also tried to prepare those who follow me so they can do the same. I'm still a serial entrepreneur, but I try to be more balanced.

In '04 I co-founded a not-for-profit organization focused on mentoring families dealing with addiction and mental illness (it seemed appropriate). Through that organization I've talked to hundreds of people of all ages, ethnicities, faiths, and backgrounds from all across the US. And I've learned some remarkable things from those people. Surprisingly, the most consistently reported lesson is one I had already learned on my own: As a group, we are remarkably grateful for both the good and bad things that have happened to us. Those trials—some of which were horrific—made us what we are today. They forced us to grow in ways that we would never have grown otherwise. We're grateful for that growth, and we all feel the need to share what we've learned.

What follows is my attempt to convey the most important lessons I've learned in the course of my lifelong education. These are the tips and tricks—the basic ground rules—for emotional intelligence that nobody ever wrote down for me. I've had to learn these lessons the hard way, and I've discovered the hard way that when you ignore these principles, you pay the price. These are the things I know now, as I approach fifty-seven, that I would have given anything to know at seventeen.

PART TWO

Lessons I've Learned About Me

CHAPTER EIGHT

Lesson No. 1

I Can't Fix a Problem
I Won't Admit Exists

On the first day my ex-wife and I went to counseling, I learned several valuable lessons. However, before I dive into those, I should probably provide some context. The time was early '83. My world was collapsing, and my inner a**hole was running wild. The counselor we were seeing was a referral from—and a friend of—my then-wife's current boss. The counselor, whom I shall refer to as Karl, also happened to be the pastor of a local church. He had agreed to see us at no charge.

We were flat broke, and we desperately needed help. Under normal circumstances, I would have welcomed Karl's offer. Unfortunately, these weren't normal circumstances. I intensely disliked my wife's boss. I thought his ethics questionable and his religion a sham. I also had a growing suspicion that he and my wife were having an affair. Consequently, I had serious reservations about anyone he recommended. I was concerned that the person he referred us to would be biased against me. The fact that his referral was a pastor made me even more suspicious. Up to that point in my life, my experiences with Christian clergy had not been favorable. So although I agreed to see Karl, I wasn't happy about it.

My assessment of what was happening between my wife and her boss would soon be confirmed. In fact, given all that would transpire over the next few years, my estimation of them would prove positively charitable. My concerns about Karl, however, were baseless. He was a man of uncommon insight and integrity. He turned out to be both extraordinarily helpful and a tremendous ally for me.

Karl started our session with introductions, getting a little background about us and setting expectations. He then surprised me by moving quickly to the heart of the matter. He asked my wife a very pointed question about something suspicious he had detected in her introductory comments. I had almost choked when she'd made that statement, so I was privately delighted that he had called her on it.

Her response to Karl's challenge was to offer more BS. Resolutely confident of her ability to charm and manipulate anyone, she went into her best Scarlett O'Hara impersonation. This was an act I had seen many, many times before. She batted her big brown eyes and sweetly presented a ludicrous explanation, lying through her teeth the whole time.

I could tell by Karl's expression that he saw right through her. Unfortunately, I misread his reaction as a complete validation of my position. This was all the justification I needed to launch into my own act. This was an act my wife had seen many, many times before: my impersonation of an atomic bomb.

My button had been pushed, and the fireball erupted. I launched into a tirade of epic proportions. I wasn't physically violent, but I was verbally crazed. My wife began to interrupt me, but Karl gently raised his hand to stop her. He made no effort at all to restrain me. He simply watched, expressionless, waiting for the hurricane that I had become to blow itself out. After some time—when I had run out of breath and out of words—it did.

After staring at me in silence for a few moments to be sure I was actually finished, Karl casually turned to my wife and asked her a question that cut me off at the knees: "Is he *always* like this?" It was both the inflection in his voice and the expression on his face that enabled this simple question to land such a fatal blow. Without uttering one word of judgment, condescension, or reprimand, Karl communicated a powerful rhetorical message: "Do you have *any* idea how foolish you look when you behave this way?"

I suddenly realized I had snatched defeat from the jaws of victory. I never knew you could lose an entire debate by being asked one question. I sat there in silence for a moment, and then attempted a recovery that only made things worse. I tried to justify my actions. Karl would have none of it. (I'll get into what I learned from that exchange in the next few chapters.)

That first session went on for two hours, during which time Karl never once let me off the hook. Toward the end, he summed things up brilliantly. He looked me right in the eyes and said, "You have a problem." He then gestured toward my wife and added:

> *She has one too, and we'll get to that later, but for right now we need to focus on you. I understand your frustration, but your verbally abusive behavior is destructive and unacceptable. You are your own worst enemy, and we're not going to get anywhere as long as that behavior continues. I need you to trust me and agree right here, right now, that we're going to tackle your problem first, or we're finished. There'd be no point in going forward.*

This statement was delivered with total resolve and with a nonverbal commitment of concern that was both powerful and humbling. He had me pinned, and we both knew it—but while I was being confronted, I wasn't being condemned. Karl's was a profoundly different approach to behavior modification than any I had seen previously. He was holding me accountable, but he was not punishing me. He was giving me a dispassionate, yet forceful critique of my specific dysfunctional behavior. He was not dismantling me as a worthless human being. Karl's arguments were based on logic and reason, not emotion. He was neither condescending nor insulting. He was clinical in his intervention, methodical and disciplined in his approach. He was so focused on my unacceptable behavior that it was as if he were trying to surgically remove a cancerous tumor. He was careful not to generalize his remarks and thereby avoided suggesting I was an unacceptable person.

Karl wasn't trying to make me wrong; he was trying to make me better. He wasn't trying to win an argument; he was trying to ensure that I won in life. And he had the wisdom to realize that if I were hell-bent on self-destruction, there was nothing he could do to save me. He was the first person to correct me while allowing me to retain my dignity. For all that he found wrong with me, he still saw and acknowledged my worth. I had not experienced that kind of attitude, sophistication, or clarity in any prior setting where I had been confronted, corrected, or reprimanded. By presenting his case the way he did, Karl made it nearly impossible for me to reject what he was saying. I would have had to be either hopelessly stubborn or incredibly stupid to reject his offer of assistance.

I agreed to Karl's conditions. We stood up. He reached out and shook my hand, and then he gave me a bear hug. In that moment, counseling stopped being about fixing my wife, and it started to be about fixing me.

This was the beginning of the end of the old me. This was also the moment I learned that the first step in fixing a problem is admitting that I have one.

I had known for years that my anger was an issue. I also knew that problems don't fix themselves and usually get worse with time. Yet I continually denied the problem, rationalized my behavior, and dismissed the objections of others. That was the downside of being too self-referencing: the only opinion I listened to was my own. Sadly, I sometimes do the same thing today. Whether I do this out of ego, pride, arrogance, laziness, or a tendency to procrastinate, I've never been quite sure. It's probably some combination of all the above. However, there's one thing I rarely talk about that I know is also in the mix: guilt.

Whenever I don't do something "right" or don't do it when or how I think I should, I feel guilty. I don't like to feel guilty, so I run from it. I also don't like it when people who don't know me or understand a situation criticize my actions. And I really don't like it when those people try to judge, condemn, or punish me in order to distract attention from their own failings.

Given that my prior exposure to religion was limited to hypocritical fundamentalists who regularly told me what an evil sinner I was, that type of judgment and condemnation was what I expected from our counselor. Curiously, that's not what I got. I thought Karl's behavior was a religious anomaly until nine months later when God showed up in my living room.

Neither Karl nor the Being I encountered acted anything like I thought pastors or God were supposed to act. I didn't get judged and condemned; I got compassion and help. There was a huge disconnect between my preconceived expectations about God and my actual experience with God. Something was wrong with this picture, and I wanted to figure out what it was.

It took me three years—the period of time between when the prediction about Claire was made and when it played out—but I eventually discovered something very interesting. *Sin* isn't a four-letter word, and it doesn't mean what most people think it means. If you look up *sin* in a dictionary, you'll find words like *evil, disobedient, guilt, wicked, wrong, immoral,* etc. All these are ideas the Bible conveys at one point or another, but none of these words matches the meaning of the biblical word most commonly translated as *sin.*

That word is an archery term. It is the Greek word *hamartia* (from *hamartanein*), and it means to miss the mark or bull's-eye. It is a statement of observable fact describing the gap between perfection and actual results. The basic idea is that if you can't acknowledge that you missed the bull's-eye, you can't start working to figure out *why* you missed it. In other words, you can't start the process of refining your aim until you admit that your aim needs to be refined. The point isn't to instill guilt or force public shaming; it's to facilitate learning. If you can't acknowledge a mistake, you can't learn from it—and neither can anyone else! I found this very interesting, but the story got better.

Most of us have seen an archery target. It's a big circle, about four feet in diameter, with five colored rings: white on the outside, then black, blue, red, and, at the center, gold. Imagine a pinpoint in the exact center of the gold circle. Hitting that tiny point is a perfect shot. Landing anywhere other than on that tiny spot is something less than perfect and is, therefore, a sin.

There are literally an infinite number of ways to sin. You can aim high, low, wide left, or just to the right. You might miss the target completely. Sometimes you know you missed the target, other times you don't. Sometimes you don't know where the target is, or if it even exists! Sometimes you miss on purpose. Sometimes you miss by accident. Sometimes you try as hard as you can and you still miss. (There's a lot that can be said about awareness and intent when it comes to sin, but that's beyond the scope of this discussion – maybe another forum at a later time.) The bottom line is this: a sin is binary. You're either on or off. You either hit perfection or you don't.

You don't have to be a rocket scientist to figure out that in archery, the standard—the bar, so to speak—for being sinless is pretty darn high. So too, it turns out, with Christianity. In His Sermon on the Mount, Jesus took a seemingly low bar that most people could step over and pushed it up one hundred miles high. He said that it wasn't enough to just not murder somebody (easy enough for most folks); now you couldn't even treat them disrespectfully!

Jesus said that calling someone a fool was a damnable offense—and this was just His opening salvo! He kept going. He took the Ten Commandments to new heights. According to Him, I *couldn't even think* about *wanting* to have sex with a woman to whom I wasn't married without sinning—pretty much all I'd been doing every three seconds since I was eleven. At this point of my understanding, I assumed I was completely screwed. But, again, the story got better.

Jesus capped this part of His sermon by explaining another binary distinction. He said that every sin is forgivable except one and *only* one. It didn't matter what else you did or how wrong you did it. In a sense, all other misses of the mark, all other sins, were equally bad, but equally survivable. You could recover from any of them—you could be forgiven and healed—as long as you didn't do this one thing. That one unforgivable sin was (my paraphrase) to deny the expertise and refuse the assistance of the one and only Coach in the universe (aka God) who is capable of reaching into your heart, mind, and soul to help you refine your aim.

A QUICK ASIDE

This declaration of there being only one unpardonable sin strikes me as an incredibly profound and enlightened statement by a Father who is infinitely more concerned with ensuring that His kids become the best they can possibly be than He is with condemning or punishing their poor behavior. It also strikes me as a very serious warning: if you don't want God's help, if you don't want a relationship with Him, He isn't going to force Himself on you. I hear that warning as a promise to leave you alone, to accept and respect your decision to go your own way. If Hell is the complete absence of God, then this warning is the ultimate expression of the admonition "Be careful what you ask for, because you just might get it."

The whole archery analogy really resonated with me because I'd grown up with real-life examples. Two of my great-uncles were rated among the best archers in the world for a period of about twenty years. They were also in the first group inducted into the Archery Hall of Fame. Archery wasn't a sport for these guys: it was a life skill in the most literal sense. They were the two oldest sons of a pioneer family with seven kids who traveled from St. Joseph, Missouri, to Southern California in a covered wagon at the turn of the last century. My uncles learned to shoot out of necessity. They had to hunt to survive. If they missed their target, the family didn't eat. So when they missed, their father didn't bother with condemnation or guilt trips. Instead, he focused on identifying the gap between actual and desired results and then closing that gap. Because their father immediately and dispassionately engaged their deficiency instead of bemoaning its presence, the two brothers were able to improve dramatically. As I heard it, the only time my great-grandfather really came down on them is when they didn't listen to his instructions. Sound familiar?

I've come to learn that blame, shame, and recrimination serve nobody. All these reactions do is drive the problems underground and cause us to hide the very issues we should be working on to fix. I've found that when I apply these reactions with others, I impede rather than accelerate their growth. And, when I apply these reactions with myself, I create a diversion that does nothing to fix the problem and only makes it worse.

Perhaps when the apostle Paul wrote, "All have missed the mark," he was conveying a novel concept. Today, however, that statement strikes me as one of the most self-evident in history. Only the severely deranged truly believe that 100 percent of their acts achieve perfection 100 percent of the time. Yet reasonable people recoil at the idea that they're sinners. I think that's because we've reduced the term to mean something it was never intended to mean.

For years, I never knew the real meaning of sin— and it has troubled me greatly to discover how many people still don't. I fear that ignorance is robbing us of the capacity to dispassionately call a "miss of the mark" what it is and then get on with the job of fixing it. I also fear it's holding us back from asking our Coach for help to refine our aim.

CHAPTER NINE

Lesson No. 2

Everything Is a Choice

As I mentioned in the last chapter, I shot myself squarely in the foot during the opening minutes of the first session with my marriage counselor. When he pointed out that fact and deftly let me know how foolish I looked, I responded by shooting myself in the other foot. I blamed my then-wife for my behavior. I said she made me so mad I'd lost my temper, and I then went on to claim that getting mad was the only way for me to confront her lies and manipulations.

Karl had a very different view:

Nobody made you do anything! She isn't holding a gun to your head, and there are plenty of other ways to confront statements you don't agree with. Maybe you don't know any other way, but you still chose how you were going to respond.

The session only got harder for me from there.

In the ensuing months and years, I came to understand that *everything* I do is a choice. Everything I consider doing but don't do is a choice. Of all the lies I've told myself, few have undermined my capacity to constructively act on my own behalf as much as this one: "I didn't have a choice."

I've discovered that I always have a choice. I have a choice to correct the bad choices I've made in the past; it's called growth. I have a choice when I decide not to correct my bad choices; it's called stupidity. I have a choice when I stand by past decisions that I still feel are right when the going gets tough; it's called tenacity. I have a choice to honor my word and commitment even when it's inconvenient or costly; it's called being trustworthy. I have a choice when I stand by my past decisions when I've been proven wrong; it's called being stubborn. I have a choice to change my choice when the known facts have changed or more information becomes available; it's called being adaptive.

I may not like the choices available to me, but I can always either opt out and forego all available alternatives, or resist the external pressure and endure the consequences. In any given situation, my alternatives may not be good. They may require me to make sacrifices. Regardless, I've learned that candidly admitting the truth behind my choices is always emotionally and relationally preferable to pretending such options do not exist. At least when I make such an admission, I'm able to demonstrate that I have the integrity and clarity of mind to call the decision what it is: my choice.

Coming in a strong second to "I didn't have a choice" is the lie "They made me…." This lie has many derivations. The one thing all these derivations have in common is that they seek to blame another for my own poor decisions.

Nobody can make me do or feel anything. (Yes, people can physically hurt or kill me, but that doesn't happen very often.) I can always resist that which I find immoral, unethical, or wrong, and I can always exercise self-control—*if* I want to. I choose how I'm going to interpret and respond to each provocation.

The real danger of telling myself either of these two lies is that in doing so (as was the case with my lame excuse to Karl), I abrogate responsibility for my own actions. Whether consciously or not, I cast myself as a victim who does not have the capacity to either control my behavior or shape my destiny. And that is a slippery slope. Pretty soon I start to see myself as a victim, and I start to see the world through a victim's eyes. I start to forget that I have the power to say yes or no. And I start to forget that I—and only I—have control over me.

Prior to '83, I saw myself as a victim. I held the unarticulated belief that I was a hostage of my family, my past, and my environment. When Karl made the statement *Maybe you don't know any other way,* he cracked open a door for me that I didn't even know existed. Until that point, I had incorrectly assumed that what I already knew was all there was to know. Nothing could have been further from the truth. Unfortunately, I didn't even grasp the possibility that there might be other tools and approaches for dealing with difficult situations that I didn't know about.

Now, I am in no way attempting to excuse my behavior, but it is a sad fact that I was acting out of my extreme emotional immaturity and ignorance. I was doing what I'd seen and experienced growing up in an ecosystem of addiction and then in the even more dysfunctional environment I created for myself thereafter. I had never had more appropriate, sophisticated, or healthier behavioral alternatives modeled for me. No one had invested in or sought to cultivate my emotional intelligence. It's not that doing so was never a priority; it was never even a concern. My brother and I have often expressed regret that we essentially raised ourselves—and we didn't do a very good job of it! Unfortunately, there are billions of people like us in exactly the same position.

A QUICK ASIDE

Nature abhors a vacuum. If one generation doesn't model and mentor emotionally intelligent behaviors, strategies, and tools for the next generation, those who follow will invent their own solutions—and their solutions, like mine, will be limited by their experience and imagination. They will be forced to reinvent the wheel, and we as a society will be forced to repeatedly suffer through the same learning curve and inefficiencies.

In a world driven by science and technology, we would never accept the premise that each generation has to start over from scratch and reinvent the transistor. How is it possible that we have failed to adopt that same attitude toward the lessons of emotional intelligence?

One of the most remarkable epiphanies I had during counseling was the realization that I wasn't a hostage to either my past or my deficiencies. Just because I'd been born into a toxic environment didn't mean I had to stay there. Just because someone said or did something didn't mean I had to respond to it. Just because I didn't know a better way didn't mean a better way didn't exist. In any situation or relationship, I had the choice of acting as my own circuit breaker. I could stop the conversation if things got too crazed or heated. I could take all the time I needed to cool down, think through my position, and seek alternatives before I responded. The game, the dialogue, could unfold on *my* time; I was not beholden to a timekeeper. I could leave anytime I wanted. I could do better anytime I wanted. This was my life. I controlled what I did and when I did it. This was a life-changing and incredibly empowering realization.

Since those counseling sessions with Karl, I've learned that failing to exercise my freedom of choice is as dangerous as failing to exercise my mind. If I don't use them, I lose them. Conversely, the more I exercise these capacities, the more I see my interactions with the world as an infinite array of choices instead of an infinite parade of dictates, and the greater becomes my capacity to consciously shape my future.

I've learned that life can be incredibly hard and people incredibly cold. If I cast myself as a victim or a hostage, I will become one, and in that state only resentment and deprivation can flourish. I've found that the first step to becoming what I'm capable of being is to acknowledge the fact that every step I take is a choice—right or wrong, perfect or flawed—that I decide, that I make for myself. I have to take responsibility for myself and own the choices I make. I can't yield that power to anyone else.

CHAPTER TEN

Lesson No. 3

Every Choice Has
a Consequence

Every action has an equal and opposite reaction. I have learned that there are consequences for every choice I make. I used to think that only bad choices led to consequences, but I've discovered that's not true. Good choices produce good consequences. I know the phrase almost seems like a paradox: *good* and *consequences* don't feel as if they should go together. But the more mindful I became of the choices I made, the more I began to realize that I had just been overlooking the good consequences. Since they didn't cause me problems, I didn't spend time thinking about them.

I also used to think that choices produced results right away. They can, but I've learned that's not always the case. Bad decisions often don't appear to be bad while things are going well. In business there's a saying:

"Revenue covers a multitude of sins." In other words, it's only when things get ugly that the consequences of a bad decision become evident.

Just like bad decisions, good decisions can take months, years, or decades to come to fruition. Sometimes the more correct a decision is, the longer it takes to prove itself correct. I've learned that this is particularly true when malicious or misinformed people have an economic or political interest in perpetuating a bad situation and are determined to block any action that would undermine their interest. I'm repeatedly saddened to see how often this actually happens.

The other really interesting thing about consequences is that they have compounding effects. The best illustration of this is interest charged against a loan or interest earned on a savings account. Consequences lead to and generate other consequences, and that compounding cycle runs perpetually until someone breaks it. The longer it takes me to recognize, admit, and act on a negative consequence, the larger the debt I have to pay off. The longer I ride the good consequences, the greater the benefit I receive.

I learned through my divorce, and in every business I've been part of since, that life presents each of us with a fundamental decision: adapt or die. The world is constantly changing. Either we change too, or we get left behind. There is no standing still. Change can be exhausting, but the alternative is extinction.

I've also learned that if you decide to change, the best way to do it is willingly and on purpose. I think of this kind of change as a conscious evolution of my mind and spirit where I chose the reality I wish to create and then take the steps necessary to bring that reality to fruition. I've learned that the best way to achieve conscious evolution is to put this principle—that every choice has a consequence—into action. It's like setting up dominos in a row or thinking three moves ahead in a chess game. I set up my future by shaping the conditions (choosing the right consequences) that are most likely to bring that future about.

CHAPTER ELEVEN

Lesson No. 4

The Only Person I Can Control Is Me

"You don't make me happy." After six years of the roller coaster that was our relationship, that was the sum total of the explanation I got from my ex-wife on the day she walked away from me forever. She ignored the fact that I was relationally crippled, lacking a clear moral compass, verbally abusive, and a recovering yet directionless drunk. Any of those would have been valid complaints, but—whether because they weren't important to her or she knew she had her own failings—none of those facts are arguments she chose.

In citing unhappiness as her reason for leaving, and in my face-value acceptance of that reason, lies the key to the emotional dysfunction and childlike logic that doomed our marriage. Neither of us was capable of either owning responsibility for ourselves or appreciating the boundary between where we stopped and the other began. I think both of us were so conditioned to see ourselves as extensions of other people, primarily our parents, that we lacked the developmental maturity to function autonomously. We weren't ready to be married. We had the rules of relationships so wrong we weren't even capable of playing the game.

I didn't begin to understand this until I shared with Karl my wife's reason for leaving. She had long since stopped going to counseling. Her stated reason was that all of our issues were my fault. I suspected the real reason was that she didn't want to be confronted. I kept going because I hoped to save the marriage, and I was beginning to appreciate the full magnitude of my problem. In this case, however, Karl pointed out to me a logical flaw that I had completely missed: This issue *wasn't* my problem! I couldn't *make* anyone happy. I could no more force happiness on another person than he or she could on me. The idea that each of us must take personal responsibility for our own thoughts, actions, and attitudes was, tragically, novel for me. I hadn't been raised to think that way.

When I was a child, my parents had total control over me. Although their influence diminished as I grew up, it was still significant until I was seventeen. Childhood requires parents to exert control over their child to ensure that child's survival. My parents and extended family told me that they knew what was best and that I had to do what they said. As a little kid, I accepted this argument as fact. As I got older, other people started telling me that they, too, knew what was best for me. Teachers, coaches, bosses, people on TV—everyone, it seemed, had a right to tell me what I ought to do and how I ought to do it.

Next I hit college and then grad school, where I got my first taste of the business world. Experts were everywhere, and it seemed that every one of them had the same basic message: "Anyone can control other people. All you have to do is be older, wiser, better, smarter, faster, or more competitive, manipulative, or ruthless." If you are strong, you lead. If you are weak, you follow. It was that simple. It didn't take me long to figure out which side of that equation I wanted to be on.

Having grown up in a culture steeped in the mythology of control, I just assumed that controlling behaviors were part and parcel of normal adult relationships. When my first wife blamed me for not being able to control her happiness, I mistakenly accepted that as a perfectly valid criticism and counted it as a failure on my part. In the fairy-tale world of my childhood and hers, I—as the man in the marriage—should have been strong. I believed I should have been the one in control. You can imagine my chagrin when I discovered I was wrong. Real strength didn't require me to take control. Real strength required me to release it.

I couldn't make my ex-wife happy. I also couldn't make her come back. You can pressure someone to get your way in the short run, but in the long run the only viable way to sustain an objective is for all parties to willingly support that objective. Gaining consensus, compromise, and agreement can be messy, but life is messy. Once I learned to deal with the mess in my personal life, I found it much easier to deal with a mess on a broader scale. And it all started with the realization that the only person I can control is me. More specifically, the only thing I can control is how I respond to the things that happen to me.

While it felt at first that I lost something when I stopped trying to control others, the reality is there are three things I gained. The first is peace. Trying to control, fix, or manipulate other people is exhausting. It was equally exhausting to try to force others to treat me the way I thought I should be treated. When I gave it up, I felt a tremendous relief. I don't know if this was the context for Ashleigh Brilliant's line "I feel so much better since I've given up hope"—but it sure could have been.

The second thing I gained is clarity. When I stopped wasting time trying to change how others lived, I was able to focus on changing how I lived. When I started to realize that I couldn't control anybody else, I began to realize that nobody could control me either. I stopped fighting needless battles. I started taking inventory of what I could control, and then I started doing those things. It began to sink in that my happiness was up to me. Other people couldn't make me happy. Only I could do that.

The third thing I gained is productivity. Once

I freed myself *from* the time-wasting exercise of controlling others, I freed myself *for* a whole host of things that I could actually accomplish. This was a bit like letting myself out of the jail that I'd put myself into in the first place.

I learned to focus only on what I can do and on what I can do well. I learned to leave the rest for others to sort out. I started trying to associate with people who shared my values and mission, and I gave up trying to control or dissuade others (like my ex-wife) when they sought to associate with people who shared their values and mission. I learned that if my values were not in sync with the values of another person's, then there was no point in trying to force the issue or the relationship. I didn't end up with the people in my life who I thought would be in my life, but I ended up much happier than I ever could have been otherwise.

CHAPTER TWELVE

Lesson No. 5

I Am What I Do

By late '83 I was becoming a therapist's dream. I was so emotionally *un*intelligent that I was a blank slate, but at the same time I was desperate to learn. A counselor could use anything from his bag of tricks with me and score a win. That said, accepting this principle that *I am what I do* wasn't easy. In fact, I hated the thought of it. It gave my hypocrisy no place to hide.

After my first wife left, I again spent some time trying to justify my behavior. Karl was never one for indulging delusional thinking, and he called me on it. He looked me in the eyes and said:

You know, you talk about a lot of things that you don't do. And you claim to be against a lot of things that you do all the time. It's like you intellectually acknowledge the existence of that chair over there, but you never sit in it. You say you're going to, and

*then you don't. You don't seem to understand that
the chair is never going to do you any good unless
you actually sit in it. Are you going to live the
ethical life you say you want, or aren't you?*

That was a tough question to ignore, and it
launched a self-examination that has lasted decades.
During that process I concluded that the way I act is
a direct reflection of the way I think. I learned that I
will never get a clearer picture of what a person believes
than by carefully observing how that person behaves in
private. We can all put on a great show in public, but
in private the real person emerges. Since no one has a
better perspective on what we do in private than we do,
we are each uniquely qualified to critically examine and
correct our own behavior. The problem is that I am not
very good at doing that, so I came up with a four-part
plan to help me improve.

First, I would acknowledge that my actions define
me in three ways. Most overtly are the things I do. Less
noticeable are the things I think I should do, but don't.
Finally, there are the things I don't even think about
doing. Each of these three can either speak well or ill
of me. It all depends on what falls into which bucket.

Second, I would call my actions what they are. I
have come to believe that most of us go to incredible
lengths to tell ourselves that we're basically good people,
but here's the problem: I can't tell myself I'm honest if
I cheat on taxes. I can't claim to have integrity if I kiss
up to a boss. I can't say I'm fair if I pretend to be asleep

when the baby is crying. I can't say I'm generous if I go out of my way to avoid the homeless guy begging on the corner. I can't say I'm forgiving if I'm holding a thirty-year grudge. I could go on and on, but you get my point: I am what I do. I needed to face that fact.

Third, I would stop rationalizing my behavior. I sometimes overlook my shortcomings because I tell myself that (a) everyone else has them too, and (b) they really aren't that bad. There are two problems with that logic. First, not everyone shares my faults, and I know it. They may have faults, but not necessarily the same ones I do—and regardless, my issues can be fixed if I want to fix them. Second, if my shortcomings really aren't that big a deal, why do they bother me? Once again, the answer isn't flattering.

I believe the negative consequences of doing (or not doing) what I feel I should (or should not) do are much bigger than I would like to admit. I have found that whenever I consciously choose to behave in ways that contradict my moral standards, my sense of duty, fairness, or obligation, I set in motion a three-part play that quickly takes on a life of its own. In Act One I fabricate stories that condemn the person I have slighted and justify my own behavior. Whatever the story, it always ends with "They do it too; they're no better than I am; they have no right to be mad at me." The story itself may be true or false, but since I never let the truth get in the way of a good story, I don't check the facts. In Act Two I repeat the story so often I start to believe it. By so doing I build up resentment over the "fact" that I'm being persecuted while the other person is not. That resentment sets the stage for the final act, Act Three, in which I give the other person what they deserve: payback!

So, in a nutshell, I invent a lie to justify my own actions; I act on that lie in righteous indignation; I punish another to deflect my own guilt; and I invite retribution from the person I have falsely accused. Viewed from this perspective, I think my rationalizations are more problematic than my shortcomings! And I think this bothers me because, deep down, I know I've lied and hurt other people because of it.

The fourth part of my plan is that once I acknowledge that my action (or lack of action) is wrong, I will change it. I think that anytime there is a problem with my behavior or with a relationship, I have three choices: admit it and start working to fix it; ignore the problem and hope it will go way (it never does; it just gets worse); or get mad about the fact that there is a problem in the first place and use that anger as a smoke screen to avoid dealing with the real issue (which, again, makes the original issue worse). Only the first of these three alternatives is productive. Anytime I fail to make the decision to change, I'm making the decision to keep things the same—which only perpetuates the problem. Conversely, if I do decide to change, I've learned to increase my odds of success by admitting to somebody else that I recognize the fact that I need to change. The mere act of doing this helps me be accountable.

As an aside, I've learned that a great choice for this

"confessor" role is the person I've victimized with my fabricated story. However, I've also learned that it's a really good idea to open my confession with an apology.

CHAPTER THIRTEEN

Lesson No. 6

I Become What I Focus On and the People With Whom I Associate

Some lessons aren't learned in a one-time encounter. These unfold over time and gradually dawn on you like a sunrise, becoming self-evident only as a pattern plays out in your life over and over again. This pattern is something I've discovered by playing the many roles I've assumed throughout my life. These roles include being a son, a hard-partying fraternity president, an academic, a husband, a patient, an ex-husband, a CPA, a father, a serial entrepreneur, a volunteer, and, ultimately, a student of faith, life, and myself. Through playing these roles I have come to realize that the longer I play a character, the more I *become* that character.

I have discovered that I have a great capacity for

talking myself into whatever it is I'm doing—no matter what that thing is. The longer I do something, the more I tend to hang out with people who do the same thing. Over time, I increasingly see what I want to see, hear what I want to hear, and find what I'm looking for. I've come to realize that the more I think about something, the longer I think about it, and the more I associate with people who think about the same thing, the more likely I am to do that thing.

I have accepted that my thoughts become my actions, and my actions become my reality. This is not so much a discipline as it is a habit. When I establish a pattern of thought, much like a pattern of behavior, it becomes hard to break. Sooner or later that pattern of thought takes on a life of its own and breaks out— sometimes without my even consciously realizing it— into action.

Thoughts and ideas are living things. They have a character and a quality that elicit both physical and emotional responses in the same way that a physical stimulus elicits a response. Thoughts and ideas create the stories that weave the narrative of my life. The stories I tell myself inspire and drive my actions, and, like actions, they also solicit internal rationalizations that work relentlessly to justify their existence. In the last chapter I described how I manufacture stories to justify my behavior. I do exactly the same thing to justify my thoughts.

This natural tendency works for me if my focus is constructive, but it works against me if my focus turns negative. Whichever way I focus, I have to stay mindful of the fact that I will soon be going there. I also have to be mindful of the people with whom I associate, because before I know it, I'm thinking just like them.

I've found that there is a somewhat unwelcome corollary to this idea: I can be focused on something or someone without ever wanting to focus on that thing or person. There have been times in my life when another person so often or so intensely subjected me to their thoughts, interests, and actions that I absorbed those behaviors without being aware of it and without wanting to do so. For example, when I was growing up, there were a few behaviors my parents had that I really didn't like, but they exhibited those behaviors so often that I internalized the very actions I loathed. I'm pretty sure I'm not alone in this.

I've learned that other people's behaviors literally imprint on me. Once that happens, those behaviors not only become habitual, they become my idea of normal. I end up doing what I hate without even thinking about what I'm doing. An example of this is children who are abused by their parents. The children undoubtedly hate the abuse, but how often do we hear of that pattern being replicated when those kids grow up and have children of their own?

If there's any lesson I should pay constant attention to, it's this one, both for my sake and my kids': I become what I focus on and the people with whom I associate.

CHAPTER FOURTEEN

Lesson No. 7

Judging People Is the Most Dangerous Thing I Do

I find there are three great advantages to getting older. First, I have so often replicated the very mistakes I have condemned other people for that I've come to realize I'm a hypocrite. Second, I have so often been presented with things I don't know that one day I realized I barely know anything. Third, after years of criticizing people for their decisions, I have so often been surprised by facts that came out later that I've come to realize I *never* know what's really going on in someone else's life. I've also been so often horrified by how wrong or unfair I was in my criticism that I've simply lost my stomach for judgment. I'm not fit to judge other people. I'm terrible at it.

The evolution in my thinking about judging

people has followed a continuum that started with condemnation, ran through correction, and then to compassion. With the great benefit of hindsight, I've found that the less mature, experienced, or self-aware I was, the more likely I was to condemn others. It was once all too easy for me to condemn that which I neither knew nor understood. It was also much easier for me to label someone than to contend with their complexities. And I can't forget the great enabler of my inner a**hole—the illusion of moral and intellectual superiority that I got from looking down my nose at those I branded inferior.

Sadly, these tendencies were always simplistic and usually wrong. I've learned that people and their circumstances are far more complex than I ever dreamed. I find that the more I ignore that complexity, the more trouble I create for myself by limiting my ability to see people and the world for what and all they really are.

The second stop in my judgment journey was correction. I came to this point after I'd gained a little life experience—but not enough to realize how little I actually had. This was the moment in my life when I assumed it was my job to set the other guy straight. This effort usually involved another over-simplification on my part, an assumption that my limited experience translated to all comparable experiences. Turns out that strategy is flawed. I may not have been completely off-base in my advice, but my advice was also not complete because my understanding of the situation was not complete. Failure to recognize that fact led me to an arrogance for which others would rightfully judge me.

The final stop of my journey was compassion. I found compassion when I realized that I can never fully understand someone else's life, circumstances, or the biology of their physical existence. By this point, I had made enough mistakes to realize that it's better to listen a lot and speak a little; better to consult than to prescribe; and better to console than to condemn.

I developed compassion when I discovered that the standards by which I judge become the standards by which I am judged—that I never win by causing other people to lose. I win by helping other people win. I win when I lay aside their mistakes and shortcomings, when I write off their debts without resentment, recrimination, or reprisal, and when I unconditionally seek their restoration, growth, and advancement so that they might do better the next time.

Compassion grew in me with the realization that just because the disaster that has befallen the other guy hasn't hit me yet, doesn't mean it won't. My compassion blossomed when I became aware of the fact that just because I didn't make his specific mistake, doesn't mean I haven't made others that were every bit as bad, if not worse. I eventually realized that compassion is the whole-hearted, unconditional acceptance of another miserably inadequate, deeply flawed human being. I had this realization when I finally appreciated that I'm as flawed as everyone else is.

True compassion seems to me to be a willingness

not to look the other way, but to look at a deficiency head-on, call it what it is, and still not hold it against the other person. I think compassion is the willingness to actively help someone overcome the calamities and carnage that they sometimes worked hard to bring on themselves without ever offering one word of condescension or derision, or without having one thought of moral or intellectual superiority. I think I will truly be compassionate on the day that I can finally behave this way consistently.

I hope I live long enough to see that day arrive.

CHAPTER FIFTEEN

Lesson No. 8

The Only Way to Fill a Hole in My Soul Is to Help Someone Else

Shortly after my first wife left, and a few weeks after my encounter with God in November '83, we started divorce proceedings. A few months after that, a guy I worked with asked me to volunteer my weekends to help build an orphanage about five miles south of Ensenada in Baja, California. I had worked my way through college doing construction, so my skills could be of use, and I wasn't doing anything at home on the weekends (other than feeling sorry for myself), so it seemed like a good idea. I never dreamed I would get out of that experience what I did.

The effort to build the orphanage was sponsored by a local Ensenada church. That church was literally dirt poor, so the only land they could get donated for the facility was way out of town, close to a dump and what looked like a small quarry. The people in the area lived in shacks made of old garage doors, corrugated metal, and cardboard. The kids had old, filthy clothes and no shoes. Many of the people looked hungry or sick. The dusty air reeked of burning trash and tires. There wasn't any electricity at the site. We had to bring down our own generators to power the tools, equipment, and lights. There was one water line. The black widow spiders that held conventions in the outhouse were big enough to ride. Going to the head meant putting your life at risk. The place was hot and humid even in the early spring, and from April through October the climate was usually miserable.

Since our time on the job site was so limited, we worked from dawn to dark and then as long as we could with the floodlights. When I first got there, the concrete slab had been poured for the foundation and the walls of the building were up, but there was no roof. My first day was spent raising the beams and framing the roof in the front of the building. We wrapped up after ten that night. Dinner was Gatorade and a couple of hot dogs that one of the guys' wives had grilled. When it came time to bed down, I grabbed my sleeping bag and headed for a quiet patch of concrete floor that had an open view of the night sky.

For the previous eight years and the last one in particular, I had spent a lot of time feeling sorry for myself. I often wished that my parents could have stayed together, that they had prepared me better for life, that

I hadn't had to work my way through school, that I had married better....The list of my grievances went on and on. But lying there on that slab, staring at the stars, I started thinking about the kids who would grow up in that orphanage. Then I started to think about the people I had seen, their living conditions and poverty, and what the long-term volunteers had told me—that the orphanage would be a huge step up in the quality of life for most of the kids who would live there.

That's when it hit me: I had never lived a day of my life without food or a roof over my head. I always had shoes and clothes and someone looking out for me. If I got sick, I got to see a doctor. I had a college education and some hope for a professional career. I had recently returned from a business trip to London and Paris where I'd flown first class on Pan Am, been a complimentary guest at the Moulin Rouge, had $2,000 dinners, and generally lived like a king. The people around here and the kids who would live in this orphanage would probably never have the kind of life or opportunities I had. I suddenly felt sick, disgusted, and ashamed. I had been so self-absorbed, so spoiled, so obnoxious, and so completely full of shit that it was appalling. I broke down and sobbed for about an hour before I fell asleep. But I'd taken another step toward managing my inner a**hole.

Perspective is a beautiful and invaluable thing. When I got up the next morning, the only thing I could think about was how grateful I was for the life I had been given and how mindful I was that my position in life was in fact a *gift*. I hadn't done anything to deserve or earn being born in a hospital in the US to educated, middle-class, white parents instead of in a dirt shack outside of Ensenada to an impoverished Mexican family. I had been phenomenally fortunate in the circumstances of my birth and the quality of my life, but I had been too blind to realize it.

When we drove home that night, I discussed my feelings with the two guys I was riding with. (We had plenty of time to talk because getting across the border late Sunday afternoon is always a several-hour ordeal.) To my surprise, they felt the same gratitude I did after working on the orphanage, and that gratitude had produced a joy and contentment that we had not even remotely imagined when we signed up to help. The act of selflessly trying to do something for somebody else, with no intention of getting anything in return, turned out to be the most rewarding and self-serving thing I had ever done. Who knew?

I have found through this and other comparable experiences that there are two ways for me to deal with grief, loss, emotional pain, and suffering: I can bury them, or I can give someone else something that will make their life better. Whenever I bury my grief and pain, I become cold and resentful. I lose joy in my life. So for me, the first option doesn't work.

Alternatively, I've found I can heal myself by going out of my way to work for the healing and restoration of others. This effort usually entails trying to give them the very thing I myself wanted but never got. I learned this by accident, but I've had the lesson repeatedly confirmed by other people who've had exactly the same experience. One of the most tangible and frequent examples of this that I regularly see is when a long-recovering addict bends over backward to help and support another addict who is just starting their own recovery. The book you are currently reading is an attempt by this recovering addict to do that very thing—to help others who are coming down the road behind me.

The most remarkable thing happens when I do something for somebody else without any ulterior motives or hope of getting anything in return: I feel wonderful about it. I feel gratitude for the fact that I was able to give rather than experiencing remorse for what I couldn't get. And the more I do to help someone who really needs it, the better I feel.

Everyone suffers loss and disappointment in life. I've learned I can't dwell on it. I've also learned I can't always prevent it. However, the one thing I can always do is to be there for a person who is suffering and do my best to try to minimize their pain.

Every time I've tried to give a gift like this to others, I've been surprised to find that I was really giving the gift to myself.

PART THREE

Lessons I've Learned About People

CHAPTER SIXTEEN

Lesson No. 9

Real Love Is Not an Emotion

I don't know when it happened, but somewhere along the line I—temporarily, at least—lost sight of the fact that love is a behavior, not a feeling. I started to believe that love is a reflexive emotion rather than an intentional action. I—as, I think, many others have—came to feel that love equates to romance and sex, falling in love, happily ever after, etc. All too often I saw love presented as the human equivalent of a male dog chasing a bitch in heat. Love was lust and infatuation.

For the longest time, I saw love as something I felt instead of something I gave. I saw love as unpredictable and fleeting instead of as something that can be invoked at will and able to endure forever. My view of love was self-focused. It was something I consumed, like firewood. The aftermath of love was something I threw away, like ash. Love was all about what I got out of the experience.

I have learned that isn't real love. Real love is a choice. It is a decision to selflessly give your very self for the benefit of another. Any time you put compassion or empathy into action to care for someone else, you get love. I have come to realize that real love occurs when you serve others.

In early 2009, at the bottom of the Great Recession, I witnessed one of the most powerful demonstrations of love I have ever seen. A married couple, close friends of ours, who had two young sons, had just lost their family business that they had struggled for a decade to build. When the financial collapse came, they were wiped out. They both worked for the business, so there was no income from other jobs—and because they had borrowed on their house to grow the business, they were also about to lose their home. Their savings were gone. They were bankrupt.

The wife had a younger sister who for several years had been sinking further into mental illness and addiction. She had robbed and repeatedly assaulted her older sister (my friend) in the past, so there was now minimal contact. For similar reasons, this sister's husband had divorced her about ten years prior and had taken full custody of their child. Since her divorce she had been arrested multiple times for crimes like possession, prostitution, and shoplifting. She had also produced two more daughters with two different men, neither of whom she married.

Each time she was incarcerated, her girls were placed in foster care. Each time she was released, she would find a way to get her girls back, go to a shelter, and then flee to another state to avoid the authorities. Her girls were abused by some of the men she serially shacked up with. She was homeless and on the streets when she called her older sister—my friend—from the Midwest and asked her sister to take in her two daughters. Both girls were ill and malnourished. The youngest was four and still in diapers; she couldn't talk and appeared to have a severe case of fetal alcohol syndrome.

Without thinking twice about their own dire financial situation, our friends got in their car and drove nonstop across country to find their two nieces whom they had never even laid eyes on. They picked up the girls, brought them home, loved them unconditionally from day one, and legally adopted them as their own children after their mother was sentenced to a long jail term.

The last thing my two friends needed in their life was the additional stress, work, and expense of two more children—especially when one had significant special needs. Due to the tremendous time required to care for the youngest child, the wife has not been able to work outside the home since bringing the girls into the family. This has only increased the pressure on them, as they have had to bear the entire financial burden for the family with only the husband's income. There is no financial assistance coming from other sources.

Of course, our friends knew full well what they

were getting into when they took in their nieces, but they willingly, immediately, signed up for all of it in order to literally save the lives of two innocent little kids. They have never—*ever*—uttered one word of complaint about the additional load this has put on them. All they talk about is how blessed they are to have the girls, how much their new brothers love them, and how well all the kids are doing. Although she still has significant developmental issues, the four-year-old who couldn't talk has recently been mainstreamed into her appropriate grade level. Apparently, a little love goes a long way!

I am humbled to tears by my friends' actions. They will forever have my respect and admiration. I don't know that I could have ever found the guts to do what they did. I'm ashamed to admit that either fear or selfishness would probably have stopped me.

Their behavior inspires me to paraphrase what the apostle Paul wrote in the thirteenth chapter of his first letter to the church at Corinth:

> *Love is patient, gracious, kind, and compassionate. It's neither selfish nor jealous. It does not brag and it isn't arrogant. Love does not seek its own betterment, but rather seeks the best in and the betterment of others. Love refuses to be provoked to anger or retaliation. Love does not take into account a wrong suffered. It does not rejoice in human failings, and it takes no comfort or satisfaction when calamity and suffering befall those who have lied, acted maliciously, or otherwise deserve it.*

Love seeks and celebrates the truth. Love gives all things regardless, relentlessly, without reservation, in spite of all the logical reasons not to give. Love bears all things, believes all things, hopes all things, and endures all things. Love never leaves; it never turns its back. Love stays right by your side, come hell or high water, forever.

I have learned that you can't necessarily choose to *feel* love, but you can always choose to *give* love. While you may be limited in terms of whom you might feel love for, you are *unlimited* in terms of whom you are able to give love to.

And that priceless gift is a gift that can change the world.

CHAPTER SEVENTEEN

Lesson No. 10

It Costs Nothing to Forgive; It Costs Everything If You Don't

've found that forgiving is a choice like any other. While the choice is easier if the offending party apologizes, I've learned that an apology should not be a prerequisite for me to forgive. My thinking on this issue has been shaped by the number of times I have judged people incorrectly and, perhaps more profoundly, by the experience I had right after my father's death. My total condemnation of him only served to further polarize our relationship. I'd held him so at bay that there was no hope of restoring our connection. And what has haunted me since the day he died is the thought that some part of the grief I felt from him after his death arose not from what he had abandoned, but rather from what I had rejected.

The conclusion I've drawn from these experiences is that the longer it takes me to forgive, the higher the price I pay for not forgiving. Said differently, the faster I forgive, the better off I am. There are five reasons why I say this.

First, what people say or do often has more to do with what type of person they are, how they think, and how they currently feel than what they think about me. I can't control whether somebody else is a jerk or having a bad day. If their behavior or perception of me is flawed, that's their problem, not mine. There is no reason for me to invest time or energy in worrying about someone else's issue.

Second, what someone is trying to say is often not what I hear. In these situations, taking offense is a waste of time because no offense was intended. After resolving miscommunications for fifty-plus years, I've come to believe that most acts to which I take offense are produced by their maker without any desire to inflict harm. The more aware I become of all the times I myself have unintentionally hurt people, the more compelled I am to forgive others when they do the same to me. I think it's unproductive for me to assume that others have malicious intent just because I don't like or understand their behavior. I've learned it's best to confirm malice before responding to it.

Third, when I fail to forgive, I keep myself focused on the past. Until my father died, I had been (at least partially) focused on the past for twenty-five years. When I'm focused on the past, I can't focus on the present—much less the future. Every offense I refuse to let go of is like an anchor on a boat. The more anchors that hold me back, the more slowly I move forward. I can't change the fact that an anchor is there, but I can cut it free. What is behind me doesn't matter anymore. Yes, it shaped me, but it doesn't need to define what I'm going to do next. I'm not hurting the other person by hanging onto history; I'm only hurting myself.

Fourth, not forgiving turns me into a victim. Voltaire expressed this idea well: "The longer we dwell on our misfortunes, the greater is their power to harm us." When I fail to forgive, I mentally replay the insult. I convince myself that people can hurt me and get away with it. I start to see myself as a victim, and eventually I become one. When I see myself as a victim, I also see myself as being entitled to behave in all sorts of terrible ways in order to avenge the wrong I've suffered. I have behaved horribly to avenge the harm done to me by others. Being a victim became my excuse to act in ways I would never think to act normally. When I did this, I hurt nobody more than I hurt myself. I damaged my image, reputation, and character. I made myself small, petty, and stupid. It was a no-win situation, and I've tried very hard not to put myself in that situation again.

Fifth, if I really believe Jesus Christ is God, then I have to accept the fact that He ordered me to forgive. Most people know about the Lord's Prayer. Most people don't realize that there is a self-directed curse in the middle of that prayer. The person praying literally prays to be punished if they fail to do what they are supposed to do.

The curse I'm referring to deals with forgiveness. Depending upon the translation, the line is either "forgive us our debts as we forgive our debtors" or "forgive us our trespasses as we forgive those who trespass against us." I originally learned the first version, but I've since discovered that what's really going on here is more profound than what either translation suggests. I've come to appreciate that the real meaning of this line is closer to "Lord, forgive us our trespasses in like measure, in exactly the same way that we have forgiven those who have trespassed against us."

To drive this point home, in His very next breath, following completion of the Lord's Prayer, Jesus says: "For if you forgive men for their transgressions, your heavenly Father will also forgive you. But if you do not forgive men, then your Father will not forgive your transgressions." I think it's a pity we don't include these last two verses every time we say the Lord's Prayer. I, for one, could use the reminder.

One more thing—and this may sound strange— few admonitions of my faith really scare me, but this is one of them. I don't fear screwing up because I know it happens to everybody, and I know that making mistakes is how we learn. I also believe I'll be forgiven when I screw up as long as I acknowledge the mistake, apologize, and work to correct it. What does scare me, however, is that I'll be hammered for my hypocrisy when I fail to forgive and accept other people. I'm not nearly as good at this as I ought to be. It's for this reason that my prayer requests tend to be much more focused on God helping me to forgive others than on being forgiven myself.

CHAPTER EIGHTEEN

Lesson No. 11

Pain Is a Prerequisite for Growth

Pain shows itself in a lot of forms. Anxiety, deprivation, disappointment, doubt, fear, frustration, heartache, incapacity, inefficiency, loss, and emotional and physical suffering are all different forms of pain. The one positive thing that all these have in common is that they force me to look inside, to search for what I'm doing wrong or what isn't working as well as it should, and to figure out ways to do things better. As necessity is the mother of invention, pain seems to be the mother of growth.

Every single time I have had a breakthrough or a period of tremendous growth in my life, either personal or professional, it was a direct result of pain. The failure of my first marriage was the most difficult thing I have ever encountered, yet it was absolutely necessary to my being able to confront my demons and ultimately become the person I am. (However much improved, I'll let others decide.) I never would have had the life, wife, or children that I have now had I remained married to my first wife.

Failures and closed doors in business have taught me how to adapt and reinvent myself professionally. Breaking my back has taught me empathy and compassion. Relational pain has given me insight and taught me the limits of what I can and should do in my interactions with another person. Relational pain has also taught me what I should accept and expect from another person in their interactions with me. Pain has taught me perseverance, resourcefulness, and tenacity. It has shown me where I've been arrogant and dismissive, and where I've judged incorrectly.

Pain has also taught me irony. I've discovered a great paradox by watching my life and the lives of many others: the road to Heaven almost always leads through Hell, and the road to Hell usually starts out looking like Heaven. Out of our greatest pain comes our greatest growth. And out of the parties that we thought would never end come our greatest self-inflicted wounds. Although these wounds are the most painful, I've learned that these "worst" things are often the best things that ever happened to us.

I've come to see that pain is soul seasoning. It's good for me. It refines my spirit and smoothes my rough edges. Pain is never fun, but I find it is often necessary. As I said earlier, I think God is much more concerned with our growth than our comfort. He doesn't always give us what we want, but He always gives us what we need—even when what we need isn't at all what we want.

The most painful periods of my life have been the times I have prayed the most. When I first started praying, I prayed what I think most people pray—that the pain be taken away. Over time and with experience, I came to pray more courageous prayers.

I believe that the most courageous prayer I can pray is this: "Lord, change me and turn me into the type of person You want me to be." I also think this is the most dangerous prayer I can pray because it's an invitation for God to bring change and therefore pain into my life.

They say you need to be careful what you pray for because you might get it. With this prayer, I can guarantee that's true—but I can also guarantee the results will be worth it.

CHAPTER NINETEEN

Lesson No. 12

Every Addiction Is an Attempt to Deal with Pain

My father was in the Air Force in the early '50s. He worked on the first hydrogen bomb projects at Sandia National Laboratory and Kirkland Air Force Base in New Mexico. He wasn't allowed to leave the United States for twenty years after his discharge, and following that he had to check in with the government anytime he left the country. After my father spent a couple of years in New Mexico, the Air Force put him someplace he couldn't talk to anyone: he was sent north of the Arctic Circle to work on what would become the Distant Early Warning system (a series of radar installations stretching from Alaska to Greenland designed to detect Soviet bombers before they could attack the US).

On one flight to a more remote installation, the wings of the plane my father was on iced over. The pilot ordered the crew to bail out, but he crash-landed the plane to try to save some survival equipment. Only one member of the crew had ever bailed out of a plane before. That guy volunteered to go first. Unfortunately, his parachute didn't open. He screamed all the way down. Another guy froze to death within forty-eight hours of the crash. The survivors dragged the two bodies with them as they started the trek to the nearest known camp.

About five or six weeks after the crash, some of the crew resorted to cannibalizing their dead to stay alive. It took two months before the Eskimos found them, and another month before they got them back to a base. During that period my father lost over eighty pounds.

My father always swore he had taken no part in the cannibalization of the dead airmen. For the rest of his life, he would have nightmares about being back on the ice and would sometimes wake up in the middle of the night yelling....

I grew up with a kid who was a genius. Late in high school he developed the first signs of what is now called bipolar II disorder. He started drinking and doing drugs to quiet the mania and forget the depression. His dad had done the same before he committed suicide in his late thirties. His son only made it to twenty-seven before he died the same way....

Over the last thirty-five years, I've seen countless other examples of people who have either been physically or emotionally afflicted. I've learned from these examples that there are three ways to deal with pain: First, acknowledge it for what it is and seek to resolve it. In the best case, this means facing the pain, learning from it, and overcoming or persevering in spite of the pain—although sometimes that doesn't or can't happen. Second, learn to live with it (not everyone can do this). Or, third, deaden the pain.

I think there are times when deadening the pain is a completely appropriate decision. However, I've learned firsthand that there are also great risks with this approach—because painkillers are addictive. I did my level best at seventeen to bury my pain in work and alcohol. I tried this approach for eight years, and the only thing it got me was a lot more pain. And I'm by no means alone in making this mistake. Most addictions are nothing more than an attempt to deal with pain that's run amuck!

I personally—and, I think, we as a society—have tended to take a very condescending and unforgiving view of people with addictions. We have not been particularly compassionate with these folks. Historically, we've looked at addiction as a moral failure, and we have ignored the roles pain and ignorance play in the rise of an addiction. It's only with recent advances in the neurosciences that we've started to realize that many of these people may more likely suffer from a biochemical, genetic, or physical disorder than a character flaw.

It's estimated that roughly 60 million Americans suffer from some kind of mental illness. These illnesses can be horrifically painful. It's not an overstatement to say that people with severe mental illness are mentally and emotionally tortured.

It's also estimated that there may be as many as 40 to 50 million Americans who suffer from severe and chronic physical pain. I'm not talking about occasional aches and pains; I'm talking about excruciating daily pain that makes you feel like you're being stabbed or that hurts so badly you can barely move. This is the type of pain that makes people contemplate suicide because they feel life just isn't worth living. As I mentioned, I've been one of these people.

If you take these two groups together, they comprise about a third of the US population, and it's estimated that half of these people have some form of addiction to drugs or alcohol. These addictions generally take root when a person is trying to deal with pain. Addictions, it turns out, are often attempts to self-medicate.

I'm not trying to excuse addicts; I want to make that clear. I am very mindful that many people suffer greatly but never develop addictions. How some people can manage and others can't, I don't know, but I do know this: it's best if I'm cautious with my judgments.

Over many years I've learned to work with an addict and exhaust all the possibilities before I close the door on our relationship. I've learned to look for the root cause before I condemn out of hand. And I've learned to remember that what drove an addict to behave the way they did toward me probably had everything to do with their pain and very little, maybe nothing, to do with the way they felt about me.

I've also learned to make clear to addicts that what they thought was a solution to their pain isn't and that their attempted solution has now become destructive to them and to me. While they're entitled to make their own decisions, so am I. And I won't support or be part of something that is going to destroy both of us. I will not facilitate their ruin or mine. They either kick their habit or I'm done. It's that simple.

Again, I've learned from firsthand experience that addicts have to save themselves. Like everything else in life, the choice of how to deal with our pain is a personal decision that each of us must make for ourselves. Nobody can make that decision for us.

CHAPTER TWENTY

Lesson No. 13

Men and Women Are Different

U ntil I was about forty, I did a great job celebrating the physical—but cursing the mental and emotional—differences between men and women. Only when Claire and I went to marriage counseling did I begin to realize that I had been wasting a lot of time and energy fighting one of the greatest gifts a relationship can offer: the opportunity to learn about a world I never knew existed.

I've come to understand that men like me live their lives half-blind. It takes most guys a long time to realize it—and some of us never do—but, metaphorically speaking, we only have one eye. Consequently, we only see part of our world; the other half is invisible. Women have exactly the same problem, but their good eye is on the other side of their head. That means the world women see is somewhat different from what their male counterparts see. I've learned that if you can bring a man and woman together (and get them to trust each other), you can significantly expand what they can see and do.

Men and women are physically wired, and socially programmed, to attend to and process information in very different ways. It's the same world: we just perceive it differently. We look at the same situation, but see two different things. We hear the same words, but interpret them two different ways. We don't use language the same way. We don't structure our thoughts the same way. Men might as well speak English and women speak French. Both are perfectly valid languages, but they are not the same. (Read Deborah Tannen's book *You Just Don't Understand* for an excellent discussion of gender language differences.)

As if these issues aren't enough, men and women don't even have the same information-gathering abilities. As but one example, women can see the entire ultraviolet spectrum of emotion, while men can only see in black and white. As a long-married man, I've come to realize that Claire picks up on things that I have no clue even exist. I now accept (at least most of the time) the fact that she sees things I can't. It only took me twenty-five years (and a lot of battles) to realize that just because I don't see something doesn't mean it's not real!

By the way, just because I use myself as an example of an intransigent learner, I'm not letting women off the hook. Women have every bit as much trouble accepting gender differences as we men do.

I'm convinced that the reason men and women argue so much about their differences is because somewhere along the line we all got the crazy idea that we're supposed to be the same. We're fighting over false expectations. We're not the same! We never have been the same. We never will be the same.

While I adamantly believe that men and women must be treated equally, I am increasingly mindful that true equality requires respect and accommodation for individual differences. In other words, I *am* suggesting that we afford the same respect to the individuality and perceptual differences of each sex; I *am not* suggesting that we treat each sex the same. For example, when a man talks to a woman, I would encourage him to try to speak to her in her language and interpret her response in the context of her language—not his. Any woman should do the same when conversing with a man.

In my marriage I've had to embrace the reality that two different languages are being spoken and to commit myself to learning the new one. It's been hard, and it's taken a long time; however, it's also improved our relationship and expanded my worldview. My wife will never see the world the way I do. I have to keep reminding myself that she's not supposed to—and that I would lose something priceless if she did.

CHAPTER TWENTY-ONE

Lesson No. 14

Human Beings Are Complex

I have two friends in investment banking that lived practically right across the street from the Twin Towers of the World Trade Center in 2001. Fortunately, they and their spouses were out of the area when the planes hit on 9/11. When the towers came down, their buildings were severely damaged.

That night, they were given a police escort and briefly allowed into their apartments to recover some personal possessions before they had to find other places to live. During those visits, both my friends—along with many other residents of the building—reported seeing firefighters ransacking the apartments and carrying off everything they liked, could drink, or could carry. To be very clear, these firefighters were not helping victims remove their valuables; they were looting. The apartment residents were yelling at the cops to do something, but none of the police even acknowledged what was happening. My friends watched the firefighters laugh over their loot and cart it off on fire trucks.

The heroes of that morning were common criminals that evening. That's an inconvenient paradox, but a common reality. And that reality of human inconsistency is something that many of us conveniently ignore. I think we do this for two reasons: first, to make it easier to condemn and dismiss other people, and, second, to excuse the inconsistency in our own behavior. I'll talk about the problems with the first now and the second in chapter 39.

I've come to believe that the word *but* should be banned from all conversations about people. I've noticed that many of us have a nasty habit of using *but* as an excuse to negate parts of other people when we see something in them we don't like: "That firefighter saved my life this morning when he ran into my office to get me, but then he stole my TV, so he's a crook." Everything that went before *but* goes right out the window the moment *but* gets introduced. The word is magical in its ability to erase one reality and replace it with another. Although it's certainly easier to label and dismiss someone than to contend with their contradictions, that practice is a dangerous oversimplification that causes a lot of problems.

Invariably, the response of the person being negated or dismissed is to resent and retaliate. None of us likes to be falsely accused or summarily dismissed. It's one thing to be called out on something you know you did wrong. The confrontation may not be easy, but most people will accept it—if not publicly, at least privately. It's a very different matter to have the thing you know you did right be condemned as a fraud, blotted out, or ignored as if it never happened. Any inclination you had to make amends for your actual mistake is likely to be suffocated by the resentment you feel for having your honorable acts dismissed or ignored as if they never happened. It's the rare individual who can graciously apologize for their wrong when the one to whom they must apologize insists on wronging them.

The fix for this problem is pretty simple. Use *and* instead of *but*: always remember that the presence of something you don't like does not negate the existence of something you do—whether in another person or yourself. Human beings are complex. Very few of our actions are black or white, on or off. Most of our behaviors fall somewhere along a continuum ranging between perfectly good and perfectly awful. There are a lot of shades of gray. Both good and bad coexist in all of us all the time. The human condition is a constant contradiction. We see the hypocrisy in ourselves—even though we hate to admit it. I think it's time we accept the fact that everybody else struggles with the issue of hypocrisy as well.

I want to stress that I'm not excusing hypocrisy or suggesting that there is no need to maintain consistency between our words and our actions. I am suggesting, however, that when we see inconsistency in another person, it is more productive to work with what is there than to throw the baby out with the bathwater. I say this for three reasons: First, if you categorically condemn a person for one behavior you dislike without showing any appreciation for an admirable quality that they also possess, you will alienate that person and significantly reduce the odds of restoring your relationship. Second, by such condemnation you show yourself incapable of a balanced assessment. You demonstrate your own immaturity, bias, and naïveté. You prove you lack discernment and the emotional sophistication to hold two equally valid, yet competing concepts in your head at the same time. Third, you make it much harder for yourself on the day (which will inevitably come) when your own behavior is inconsistent, the tables have turned, and you want someone to accept you.

CHAPTER TWENTY-TWO

Lesson No. 15

Everybody's Got Something

I've come to believe that everybody—every single person I will ever meet—has some area of brilliance, some God-given talent, some gift and capacity for true genius that is nothing short of breathtaking. It may not be immediately evident, but it's there. I just have to look for it.

I think we've fallen into the nasty habit of evaluating others based upon whether we see in them that which we value in ourselves. In other words, if you're an athlete, you judge others based upon whether they share your physical prowess. If you're a mother, you judge other moms by how creative or well behaved their kids are. If you're a conservative, you judge liberals harshly, and vice versa.

It seems to be perfectly acceptable these days to dismiss those who don't share our capacities, interests, or outlook. We write people off and ignore them because they are not like us.

I have found this kind of behavior to be both personally and professionally disastrous. When I behaved this way, I made two mistakes. First, I failed to see what I needed to see to either keep myself out of trouble or to make the most of my opportunities. Second, I failed to recognize that I needed to see more at that moment than I could. In other words, I didn't even realize that my lack of vision was a problem. After many painful lessons, I've come to believe that there is a very self-serving reason why I need to appreciate people who are different from me instead of dismissing them. It's called *self-preservation*. Let me give you some examples.

Had the *Titanic*'s captain realized he needed to see more than he could see, you never would have heard of the ship. There were spotters in the crow's nest the night the ship hit the iceberg, but they could only see so far. Their physical field of vision was limited. There are reports that those spotters communicated their concerns about their limited vision up the chain of command, but their captain dismissed them. He appreciated neither the limitations of his crew nor his requirement to be able to spot danger at a greater distance. Without a more complete field of vision, the entire ship met with disaster.

I think that we, too, need to realize that our field of vision has both physical and psychological limits to what we can see and appreciate. We all have these limitations to what we can see and appreciate because we all have different strengths and interests, and those differences cause us to focus on different areas.

I did not appreciate this fact when I co-founded my first company. Neither did my co-founders, who shared my background. We did not have the right talents or team around us to take a good idea and turn it into a great company. We were a team of people who all played the same position. (Not a good idea in a sport; also not a good idea in a business.) We had one perspective: we had the coolest technology in the world. What we failed to realize is that nobody cared about our technology. They only cared about the results we produced and how easy those results were to achieve.

Had our team had the benefit of a marketing or sales strategist who understood the customer's mind-set, we would have been able to sell our company a year or two before we did. The difference in timing would have meant another $10 to $15 million in my pocket.

The necessity of appreciating the different talents of others was an expensive lesson for me to learn—and it's not one I'm ever going to forget. In fact, I'm convinced that as we navigate the great ocean of life, the most vital determinant of our success will be our ability to surround ourselves with a team of people who have wildly different interests and talents than we do, who can see and appreciate things that we can't, so they can warn us before we hit the iceberg. Otherwise, we're going to sink a lot of ships.

CHAPTER TWENTY-THREE

Lesson No. 16

People Will Tell You Who They Are; You Need to Listen to Them

I've discovered you can learn a lot by watching and listening to people. I think the problem most of us have is that we don't believe what we see and hear. Remember the idea that you are what you do? Well, that principle applies to other people too: they are what they do.

People are creatures of habit. Once they've worn a rut, they tend to stay stuck in it. The deeper the rut—the longer someone has been in it—the harder it is for them to get out. Of course, people can change, and they do. But they change slowly, they do so imperfectly, and they suffer setbacks along the way. When determining whether to start or stay in a relationship, I've found that is a good thing to keep in mind. I've learned not to ignore what went before in that person's life, because when it comes to human behavior, the past is a pretty good predictor of the future. I've also learned that if something feels wrong about a person, it probably is!

I've found that if people lie, cheat, steal, or do things that are immoral or illegal, I need to walk away. If they did it once, they'll do it again. If they've done it to others, they'll do it to me. If they tell me that they think it's okay to "F" somebody over to get what they want (as one of my old bosses did), I now take them at their word. Unless they are obviously joking, people rarely make outrageous statements they don't mean. And it's not too difficult to determine whether they're joking. You usually just need to ask.

Whatever issues I see in the early part of a relationship, I now assume I will see more of the same later. People can only stay on their best behavior for so long. Conversely, if someone is kind, fair, honest, open, responsible, and generous, I can expect that those are qualities they value. I will probably see more of the same going forward.

What I tend to forget is that, at a deep level, people do what they value. If we engage in a given behavior at all, there is invariably something inside us telling us that such behavior is either okay or it serves us in some way. We all get something out of everything we do, or we would never do it. While that fact doesn't necessarily speak very highly of all our own behaviors, I think it is an incredibly important thing to keep in mind when I listen to what other people are telling me about themselves.

PART FOUR

Lessons I've Learned About Relationships

CHAPTER TWENTY-FOUR

Lesson No. 17

The Only Difference Between Me and My Parents (or My Kids) Is the Number of Years Between My Birth and Theirs

When I was in college, I had a friend whose dad had the best relationship with his kids of anyone I had ever met. He treated them as peers, not as property. He advised and instructed. He coached. He never relinquished his authority, but he did listen to their input before determining what to do. He was collaborative, not authoritative, in his decision-making process.

This dad was both personally and intellectually approachable. He did not presume to have all the answers. Instead, he focused on teaching his kids how to ask the right questions and find the answers on their own. When he made a mistake, he admitted it and sincerely apologized. He never acted like a martyr or resorted to guilt trips and manipulations to get his way.

He and his kids shared a mutual respect. He sought their growth and advancement over his own comfort. His kids went overseas during college, and he missed them terribly, but he pushed them to go because he wanted them to learn. He sought the benefit and best for his kids in spite of the discomfort or loss that he might experience. His kids adored their dad because he had modeled for them what it meant to truly love.

I had not experienced anything like this in my relationship with my own parents, so I asked him what his secret was. What follows is my best recollection of his response, coupled with a few of my own twists that I've added over the years:

> *Even as an adult child, I have to remind myself that my parents have no special powers over me. They don't own me. They never did. They are not inherently better or smarter than I am. Their control over me lasted a short period of time.*
>
> *I have to keep in mind that while I was growing up, my parents were wrestling with many of the same issues that I wrestle with today. They were no better equipped to deal with those issues*

than I am now. In fact, they were probably far more poorly equipped than I am. They made mistakes, like I do today. Even if they didn't grasp their shortcomings then, they probably do now. And I'm sure they feel as bad about their mistakes as I do about mine.

As a parent, I need to keep in mind that I have no special power over my children, and any power I do have won't last long. I did not create them; God did. I do not own them; God does. I am not inherently better or smarter than my children are. As people, they are my equals. They deserve respect in the same way that I deserve respect. I am nothing more than one-half of the physical equation by which their bodies came into existence. One day they will repeat that process. And one day both my body and theirs will return to the dust from which it came.

As a parent, I am only my children's coach for a little while. It has been my job to love, protect, and prepare them for their future as well as I possibly can. When they were young, there were lots of things they hadn't been exposed to yet. They were temporarily ignorant; they were not stupid. I tried to never treat them as if they were, and to constantly keep that distinction in mind.

Metaphorically speaking, I tried to always throw the ball over their heads and make them jump for it. I talked to them like adults when they were infants. I expected that they were smart *and able to understand; I tried, not always successfully, to patiently explain if they didn't. I tried to be transparent about my own questions, to be open about my mistakes, and to apologize to my children when I was wrong. I tried to model that it is okay to fail as long as you always try to fix the mistake.*

It took me years to even begin to embody the concepts and postures of parenting that were conveyed to me in the words above. Internalizing these principles was a struggle at which I failed more often than I succeeded. Only at the end of the years when my kids were at home did I finally begin to become the parent I wanted to be. Through that process of fits and starts, introspection, reflection, and exhaustion, I came to one conclusion: the only real difference between parents and children is that one party started off down the road of life a few years before the other. All that means is that one has experienced more of that road than the other. That experience can be tremendously valuable, but if it is not shared with candor and humility, it will be wasted.

I see myself today as but one link in a very long chain. However, within that chain each link plays a pivotal role. Whatever family dysfunction has befallen any of us in the past, it is within our power to end it in the present. Patterns of poor behavior are often passed down from generation to generation. I have made it my goal to ensure that the negative patterns from my past will stop with me. No doubt I will miss some problems and invent others. No doubt every generation will do the same. However, if we all adopt this goal to ensure that negative patterns of behavior stop with us, we will probably improve the well-being of our descendants for centuries to come.

I've taken the challenge to improve my emotional intelligence and ensure that the world I leave my kids is better than the world my parents left me. Now the question is, will you?

CHAPTER TWENTY-FIVE

Lesson No. 18

Always Invest in Others As Long as They Invest in Themselves

When I was about nine, my eldest cousin married a guy from San Francisco. My new cousin-in-law's dad was in his fifties at the time, and he was the only adult male in our extended family who treated my brother and me like we were human beings. For that, we idolized him.

He was a fun guy to be around. He had a great sense of humor and little tolerance for the posturing and social-climbing BS for which some in my family were famous. He worked on the San Francisco docks as a longshoreman, but he had been born in Philadelphia. His mother had died during the flu pandemic of 1918, leaving him at the mercy of an alcoholic father who—in his words—"used to regularly beat the hell out of me."

At thirteen he began to fear for his life, so he dropped out of school and ran as far away as he could. He eventually landed in the Bay Area. The man was brilliant and probably could have been wildly successful if he had ever been able to finish school. Unfortunately, that's a tough thing to do when you're homeless and alone from the time you're thirteen.

One evening when I was in college, I was leaving a construction job that was close to where he was staying, and I called him up to see if he wanted to have dinner. He was free, so I grabbed a pizza and headed over. We spent hours that night talking about things we'd never discussed before. He knew all about my dad leaving, that I was supporting myself and putting myself through school. That was the first time he told me about his background and having to run from his father. Suddenly my situation didn't seem so bad.

We talked a lot that night about a lesson he'd learned decades before that I was just beginning to grasp. The lesson dealt with having gratitude for the little things, the gifts in our lives that we might otherwise take for granted, and our unwillingness to waste those gifts on people who didn't share our appreciation of them.

During our conversation, he gave me a couple of illustrations of this principle, but one struck close to home. He talked about raising his son and how hard he had tried to support him as he pursued his interests. This dad had just one ground rule: as soon as his son lost interest in something, Dad pulled his support. He felt he had worked too hard to waste what he had earned. If his son wasn't willing to take something seriously, then he wasn't either.

He ended his illustration with a proof-point and a caveat. Both were compelling. As evidence that his child-rearing strategy had worked reasonably well, he reminded me, with more than a little pride, that his son was a nationally known scholar and author. But then he cautioned me to confirm that the person in whom I was investing had actually lost interest before I withdrew my support. He told me about one time his son had wanted to take piano lessons, so he bought a piano and hired a teacher. After a little while his son said he didn't want to take lessons anymore. His dad said, "fine." The next day, when the son came home, the piano was gone. His dad had sold it.

What he (the dad) later discovered was that his son still wanted to play the piano. His son had only asked to stop taking lessons because the teacher's breath was so bad "it could knock a buzzard off a shit wagon at twenty paces." His ten-year-old son was getting physically ill smelling this woman's breath. He couldn't stand it any longer, but he was too embarrassed to say anything. The father's comment to me was "I kind of blew that one. Don't you make the same mistake."

Over the decades, I've had plenty of opportunities to think about this rule and its implications. I've come to believe that you can't give someone too much love and support as long as your gifts are appreciated and put to good use.

There are three reasons why I believe this and why

I made it my mission to teach my kids the mantra *I will invest in you as long as you invest in yourself.* First, the unspoken message your love and support sends to the person you are assisting is incredibly valuable for the bond between the two of you and for their sense of self-worth. The world spends a lot of time tearing us down. A little kindness can make a big difference in giving someone the courage to stand up to the world's wrecking ball. The investments you make may not seem like much to you now, but I've found that the people in whom those investments are made often remember them for a lifetime. I know I have.

Second, by modeling the behavior of giving for someone we care about, we encourage them to do the same for other people they care about. This has a ripple effect that multiplies the impact of the gift in both current and future relationships. By investing in other people today, we are investing in the relationships and lives of tomorrow.

Third, giving is good for the giver. I've learned that investing in others builds my own character. Nothing helps me become more grateful for what I have than when I start giving it away to those who may not have as much. I actually wish I were better at going out of my way to invest without conditions or reservations.

Now, having said all of the above, I must reiterate the one ground rule: when your investment in another person is no longer appreciated or is intentionally squandered, it's time to stop giving. There is a fine line between supporting someone's efforts to achieve their full potential and enabling their dereliction of responsibility or inviting their disrespect. If I continue to give support when it's not appreciated, I'd better be prepared to confront the fact that I'm enabling them for my benefit and not theirs.

CHAPTER TWENTY-SIX

Lesson No. 19

If There's Ever a Conflict Between Doing the Legal Thing and the Loving Thing, Choose the Latter

I n '87 I joined a privately held med-tech company. One of the senior executives in that company was a crusty "old" guy named Carroll. (When I met Carroll, he was in his late forties, which is younger than I am now. Maybe he wasn't so old after all....) A former Navy pilot, he had served two tours in Vietnam, flown scores of missions over Hanoi, and been shot at more times than he could count. He used to talk about flying with a bottle of Jack Daniel's between his legs because, he said, if he was going to die anyway, he figured he "might as well be comfortable."

He got out of the Navy after his kids were born and went into sales. He climbed the corporate ladder and now ran about half our field operations. He was a road warrior. He smoked too much, and he definitely knew how to drink. He scared the hell out of me, and I haven't said that about many people.

I did all the financial planning for our company, and Carroll regularly disputed my forecasts in a very public fashion. His favorite opening line— usually delivered in front of the entire leadership of the company—was "I was wondering if you would like to tell us what kind of pot you were smoking when you put this plan together—because there's no way in hell a sober person could come up with this shit." And that was the delicate lead-in! His assault on my character, intellect, and breeding ramped up significantly from there.

In early '90 I had to join Carroll on a trip to Seattle to finalize a minor business acquisition. I was not looking forward to it, but it turned into one of the most pleasant surprises of my life.

The woman who owned the company we were buying was a nurse by background. She knew healthcare, but she knew little about business. Carroll was a pro who could have easily run circles around her. I expected him to drive the hardest bargain imaginable, take full advantage of his expertise over her naïveté, and, basically, steal the business from her. After all, this was a business transaction, and he, as an officer of a now publicly traded company, had a fiduciary responsibility to our shareholders to secure the best deal possible.

In public accounting I had worked with lawyers and investment bankers on close to twenty much larger business sales. These three professions (accounting, law and banking) can be ruthless. They tend to follow the letter of the law to get the best possible deal for their clients, regardless of who they have to destroy to get there. With their "me first, screw you" philosophy, humanity rarely factors into the equation. The only thing that counts is the financial bottom line. That philosophy never sat well with me, but that's the way it was, and I assumed I had to live with it. I thought this transaction would be the same. It wasn't.

We arrived for the first meeting at about 10 AM, went through the introductions, and got to work. From the outset, the tone wasn't what I expected. The company's owner was very defensive and guarded. (I assumed she was afraid we were going to take advantage of her, and I considered such fear appropriate.) However, Carroll, instead of negotiating for everything he could get, was bending over backwards to be fair. There were several occasions where she either suggested something that would actually work to her detriment, or she was ready to agree to a term that our attorneys had drafted that would have hurt her. In each case, Carroll stepped in to save her. He would calmly explain why this wasn't a good idea and how it could be a problem. He would then offer a more balanced alternative that would achieve the same objective but do so in a non-punitive fashion.

At first I thought he was just trying to establish rapport or lull her into a false sense of security. But that wasn't what he was doing. I didn't really get it until we wrapped up the first day's session late that evening. As we were leaving, she thanked him for being so evenhanded. She admitted her surprise that this was the case. He came back with something I had never heard before during a negotiation:

> *There's no need to thank me. I'm just looking out for myself. We're not conducting a transaction; we're establishing a relationship. We're going to work together for years to come. It's in my best interest—and the company's—to be sure that this relationship is fair, that it will endure, and that it will provide you with the resources you need to properly take care of our patients and customers. This relationship has to work for everybody, or in the end, it will work for no one. If it doesn't work, I'm going to have to spend time to fix it, and that will end up costing more money than if we just got it right in the first place. Since I'm basically lazy* (he said smiling), *I'd rather get it right the first time.*

What Carroll said made an incredible amount of sense, both ethically and economically, but until that moment, I had never been introduced to this way of thinking. Accountants, lawyers, and investment bankers are generally mercenaries. They don't care about relationships, because they never stick around to deal with them. Relationships are somebody else's problem. These professions tend to focus overwhelmingly on today and largely ignore tomorrow. Sadly, this "grab all you can get today and don't worry about tomorrow" perspective has permeated American business and has become an unwritten rule that, for a long time, I just accepted without question.

Our society creates a lot of rules like this one, and many of us (myself included) feel some obligation and pressure to adhere to these rules. Sometimes when we follow the letter of the law instead of the intent, when we do what is expected instead of what is compassionate, or, most importantly, when we focus on the right now instead of the long term, people get hurt. Their voices and rights get crushed, their humanity gets marginalized, and their interests get cheated. Anytime that happens, there are negative consequences. People hate to be cheated, and it's just a matter of time before, whether consciously or not, they try to get even. Carroll understood this. At that point in my life, I didn't.

Most business people would have expected Carroll to aggressively pursue the best economic deal he could get upon the signing of the contract. If you evaluate the financial arrangement based solely on the execution date of the agreement, he didn't do this. However, if you take a longer view—if you extend the time horizon to include the duration of the relationship that was being memorialized by the contract—he did. He saw the difference between paying the lowest price today and incurring the lowest costs over time. In business parlance this is called Total Costs of Ownership (TCO). Carroll designed this contract to ensure that our company would incur the minimum possible cost and realize the maximum possible profit over the life of the relationship.

Over the last twenty-five years, I've discovered a relational equivalent to TCO. The idea is exactly same: get the most out of a relationship with the minimal amount of pain. Like TCO, the concept is focused on the long term instead of the right now, but unlike TCO I've found it easier to achieve because the criteria on which I need to focus are more limited.

Carroll taught me that if I'm ever in a position in which I'm trying to figure out what to do about some rule, I have to ask myself just two questions: If I were in the other person's shoes, how would I want to be treated? And what would I regard as fair? I can't let myself off the hook by throwing in words like *but* or *except*. I can't fall back on precedent because what came before doesn't always matter. The fact that I haven't experienced something doesn't matter. The fact that I haven't seen something doesn't mean it's not real. Maintaining or gaining power doesn't matter. Getting the most today is not nearly as important as getting the most over a lifetime. And doing what others expect me to do should have the least bearing of all on my decision.

The older I get, the more convinced I become that

the only things that do matter in these situations are the principles of fairness, equality, compassion, and love. It seems that when I make these the true north of my moral compass, I never lose my way. And, when I apply these standards, whatever answer I come up with, that is what I need to do because, in the long run, that is actually the most self-serving thing I can do.

CHAPTER TWENTY-SEVEN

Lesson No. 20

If a Friend Tries to Give You Constructive Criticism, Listen

After my dad left, people tried to talk to me about my anger. I ignored them. My life got worse. When I was in college and grad school, peers and professors took me aside and tried to talk to me about my destructive behaviors. I ignored them. My life got worse. My brother tried to talk me out of marrying my first wife. I ignored him. My life got worse. Finally, in marriage counseling with my life in ruins, I started to listen to people who were obviously trying to help. My life got better. By the time I went on the business trip I just described I knew there was value in listening to people. That was good because Carroll had more to teach me.

To continue the story where I left off, at the end

of the first day's negotiations, Carroll and I had dinner at the hotel bar. Shortly after we sat down, we had company. A lone woman who was about my age came up and sat one seat away from me. She was obviously on a business trip. She had her papers spread out in front of her and was working while she drank. She was chatting me up from the time she sat down. (I hadn't been out of the dating scene so long that I had forgotten what it was like to get hit on, as rare as that occurrence was.) As the drinks and evening went on, she became a bit more direct. She eventually leaned over to me and suggested in a whisper that we go back to her room. Carroll may not have actually overheard her, but he knew exactly what was going on. I politely, but rather firmly, said, "Thanks, but no. I'm married and intend to stay that way." She said something like "Oh well! Your loss!" and then packed up and left.

Only after she was gone did Carroll say a word. "You could have gotten lucky tonight," he said with a grin. I knew that many of the salespeople in our company were about as morally compromised as they could get, and I fully expected Carroll to be the same. I was sure that he was about to give me grief for not cheating on my wife. As I braced for the hazing that I thought was about to follow, I told him I didn't believe in adultery. I had seen what it does to families, and I wasn't going to do that to my kids. I said it with a real tone of disgust, trying to let him know what I thought of people who behaved that way. In essence, I was sending the first shot across the bow in the debate that I thought was about to follow.

That was the second time that day I misjudged Carroll. He surprised me again by saying, "That's good, because I would have killed you if you'd gotten up to go with her." My head snapped around, and I looked at him with an expression that said it all. I couldn't believe what I was hearing. *Was he joking?*

He came back and said, "You thought I was going to condone that behavior, didn't you?" I said, "Truthfully, yes." He continued, "You even expected me to give you a hard time because you turned her down"—to which I replied, "Yes, I did." He said, "Well, I wouldn't have. There's a fundamental law of the universe. If you cheat on and lie to your spouse, you'll cheat on and lie to anyone. I have no tolerance for people like that, and you, my friend, just passed a test."

Friend? I thought to myself. *You must be kidding.* At this point I was thoroughly confused. This guy either wasn't who I thought he was, or he was playing games with me. It turned out to be the former, but I only came to that conclusion after several hours of the increasingly candid conversation that followed.

As it approached closing time, I finally summoned the courage to ask Carroll a question that had been brewing for hours. "So, if you're not such a bastard, why in the past have you so publicly beaten me up?" His response—and I paraphrase from memory—was:

> *A couple of reasons: First, it's my job to look out for the people who work for me. I have to be their*

advocate and bring to your attention—forcefully, if need be—the reality of what goes on in the field that you can't possibly know about when you're stuck in the corporate office. Second, you've come off with the arrogance and swagger of a guy from Wall Street, and that hasn't sat well with a lot of us little people. You're very intelligent and well educated, but you presume and prescribe instead of conferring and collaborating. I know you've been groomed to behave that way, but you haven't quite come to understand that it doesn't serve you well. To your credit, you're beginning to. And people are also beginning to figure out that there's a decent human being inside you. I've seen more proof of that today. There's definitely hope for you yet. You just need someone to kick you in the ass a little more often to bring it out.

He got a big grin on his face, slapped me on the back, raised his glass to finish off his last Scotch of the night, and said, "And I'm just the guy to do it."

I suddenly realized I was being educated by a master! His assessment was accurate, and I knew it. From that night on until the day he died, Carroll was a dear friend and mentor. He constantly kicked me in the ass, but he also taught me a lot about managing my inner a**hole. I thought the world of that guy.

Through this experience and others, I've discovered that even when a wrongly suspected enemy criticizes me, I must accept the fact that there is probably some truth in the attack. Foes may say things that are completely groundless just to hurt you. However, since we all know that arrows hurt more the closer they get to the truth, a really good critic will pick an actual weakness and present it in the worst possible light. Their comments may not be fair, but they may be accurate. They may not be trying to help, but they may be providing valuable feedback.

Nobody likes to get criticized. It hurts, and it can be humiliating. It can feel like failure. We all have the propensity to take criticism badly. Although some of us can absorb it better than others, nobody actually likes to get bad news. We all know that.

So, when someone who obviously cares about me (a mentor, my wife, a friend) takes the risk of making me mad or injuring their relationship with me in order to give me some feedback they know I don't want to hear, I've learned to sit down, shut up, and listen. If they bumble the delivery or come up with bad illustrations, I just have to be patient and not react. In those moments I try to remember that they are probably nervous and would rather be somewhere else. I know that none of us are at our best when we hate what we're doing. What they're saying may be hard for me to hear, but it may be equally hard for them to say. I've found that the worst thing I can do when someone is trying to give me constructive criticism is to be formulating my response while they are talking. I try (not always successfully, mind you) to force myself to really listen to what they are saying instead of listening to the barrage of excuses and explanations that are popping into my head. If I'm talking to myself, I can't hear the other person's message.

I have also learned not to interrupt the person giving me feedback, and to let them get it all out before I say anything. If I don't let them finish, the message I send is that I'm more interested in defending myself than in becoming a better person or improving our relationship. When I have confirmed that they have finished speaking, *then* I can ask questions.

What Carroll did in the story I just shared was brilliant: he used *and* instead of *but*. He took my measure and found me wanting, but he did not find me worthless. That was a simultaneously humbling and comforting assessment. I find that I, like most other people, respond better to that kind of balanced approach that acknowledges both the right and the wrong.

Conversely, if someone comes to me with feedback that ignores all things positive and focuses entirely on the negative, I tune them out, because it's obvious that they are more interested in pursuing their own agenda than helping me grow and improve as a human being. These people also lose credibility in my eyes because they've shown themselves incapable of seeing the entire picture. That loss of credibility is a shame for both of us, because it means that neither of us takes away from the interaction what we could have.

CHAPTER TWENTY-EIGHT

Lesson No. 21

The Message Behind the Message Is Usually More Important Than the Words

Two chapters back, I shared the story about how Carroll interacted with the woman whose business we were about to buy. If you recall, she was guarded and defensive, but he was magnanimous. While their conversation focused on the contractual terms by which we would acquire her business, Carroll's non-verbal communication focused on what she could expect from her soon-to-be employer.

Each time Carroll stepped in to save the company's owner from agreeing to a contractual provision that would have been to her detriment, he was sending several messages. The first was that he knew what he was doing. By inference, she did not, but by never calling that out, he allowed her to maintain her dignity and to arrive at her own conclusions about their relative levels of business expertise. He was showing her he was gracious.

The second message Carroll sent was that he was not going to use his knowledge to gain an advantage over her. He was going to use his knowledge to create advantages for both of them. He was putting their team above himself, and showing her that collaboration and "winning together" were ethics he valued.

His third unspoken message was that he was much more interested in fairness and the long-term health of their business relationship than in any short-term personal victory. Even though he never once uttered a word along those lines, he was methodically building a foundation for their relationship—a foundation of trust, respect, integrity, consistency, and dependability.

Two entirely different dialogues played out that day. When I was young, I was so literal I would have missed the second dialogue. I used to focus exclusively on the words being spoken during a conversation, and I would ignore the messages behind the message. I would not pay attention to the context in which the words were used, and I would give no thought to the implications, timing, or nuance of a statement. Subtlety and innuendo were lost on me. This inability of mine to appreciate the entire conversation served me poorly for two reasons.

First, other people don't always use words the way

I do. Some people attach different meanings to the same word. Others say things they know aren't true or don't believe because they have ulterior motives or feel they must maintain some party line. Still others paint pictures with words. They use words more as an expression of a feeling than the meticulous specification of an idea. When I have failed to keep this fact in mind, I have misinterpreted much of what was said. I have sometimes heard what other people didn't say, missed what they were saying, and reacted to what they didn't mean. This was not a recipe for success.

The other reason my failure to recognize the second dialogue was a problem was that I missed the more important message being communicated by the person's actions. When I did this, I lost out on the chance to listen to the nonverbal messages that would either corroborate or contradict a person's words. I did not yet realize that in any conversation, much like in a stereo soundtrack, at least two distinct messages are always being communicated.

I learned early on that people don't always mean what they say. I learned later that they almost always mean what they do—at least in the long run. I've discovered that the message communicated by people's actions is the one to which I need to listen. It is also their actions, not their words, to which I need to respond.

Another great illustration of this principle is—as I described in the last chapter—listening to a friend who offers constructive criticism. I've lived out this example more times than I can count, and I have handled it badly many of those times. I've had to learn to listen to both of the messages my friends and family were sending. In the first message, their words are usually trying to explain a better way for me to do something. In the second message, their actions are trying to tell me they care about me. They're trying to show me that they want what's best for me and that they want me to be the best I can be. When I keep the second message in the forefront of my mind, I find it a lot easier to hear and appropriately respond to the first.

CHAPTER TWENTY-NINE

Lesson No. 22

Anger Kills Dialogue

We all get frustrated from time to time, but just because I'm frustrated doesn't mean I have to get mad. I've learned that, as with everything else, I have a choice about how to handle frustration. I can calmly and respectfully resolve it, or I can launch into an angry outburst or try manipulation to get my way. This chapter is about the dangers of the latter. As I explained in the first part of this book, I know this issue well. Of all the lessons I've had to learn the hard way, I am most ashamed that I had to learn this one.

I have found that anger kills a conversation and a relationship faster than almost anything imaginable. Anger shows up in two forms: active and passive. These have different characteristics, but are both usually provoked by uncontrollable events that are perceived to either question a person's competence or authority or undermine their security. In both cases, the objective of the anger is also the same: shut down the threat and make the problem go away. That tactic may work temporarily, but it always fails in the long run.

Active anger is the traditional, violence-prone rage. It is overt. These are drunks who want to fight over a perceived insult, guys who beat their wives for questioning their authority, and bosses who throw temper tantrums because a project isn't going well. These people scare and intimidate to get their way. They are bullies. I want to get away from these people for my physical safety.

Passive anger is the opposite: it's covert. This is the martyr act, the "Poor me; you're always right; I'm always wrong; you're always picking on me" defense. This approach takes a valid criticism and turns it into an absurdity that no reasonable person would actually suggest. The next words out of the mouth of the person who initiated the criticism are usually "That's not what I meant, and you know it." I want to get away from these people because I can't stand the frustration.

I've found that both forms of anger send two unspoken messages. First, the person getting angry believes that it is okay to either abuse or manipulate the person with whom they are angry. Second, the person getting mad is unwilling to hear the other person out and seriously work to resolve the problem they brought to the table. Both of these messages imply that the person who is the focus of the anger is unworthy of respect.

These are condescending and insulting messages. Unfortunately, since the messages are unspoken, they also tend to be unconscious. So while the emotional content of the messages registers, neither the sender nor the recipient is usually able to articulate exactly what just happened. Consequently, in the aftermath of an angry outburst, the target of the anger usually either shuts down and pulls away or retaliates. In both scenarios, the issue that has surfaced does not get resolved, the problem festers, and the two parties are further polarized.

The longer the issue goes unresolved, the more the pressure builds. Eventually the problem and the person will not be silenced any longer, and the issue resurfaces. However, this time it has more energy behind it. Resentment is driving it forward. What could have been peacefully resolved earlier is now a much bigger deal. Having been shown contempt before, the offended party is less likely to accept that treatment again. Emotions escalate, and simple, peaceful solutions become harder to find. This is how wars start.

Anger causes isolation and a loss of opportunity. When I get angry, I lose the chance to show someone respect. I lose the chance to hear their perspective and the information they have to share. I lose the ability to leverage their talents and resources. I lose my relationship with them. I lose the chance to learn, to see what's really going on, and to head off little issues before they become big ones. And as a result I lose time, energy, and the hope for what could have been.

I have learned over the years that anger has malignant ramifications. It causes resentment that lingers long after the outburst is over. Anger quickly destroys trust and intimacy, and it leaves emotional wounds that take a long, long time to heal. Anger doesn't just kill the open exchange of information in the short term; it can kill it for years to come. Sometimes anger even kills communication permanently.

I have come to believe that, although regrettable, defensive anger is sometimes required. There are times when I may have no viable alternative other than to defend my life or the lives of others. On the other had, offensive anger—where I am the instigator and aggressor—is always my choice. It is never required and never justified in a relationship. I never win when I try to make the other guy lose.

CHAPTER THIRTY

Lesson No. 23

You Don't Have to Fight Back

I learned this trick from Karl, the marriage counselor who worked with my ex-wife and me. She was masterful at pushing my buttons. I was masterful at responding each time my buttons were pushed. After watching this pattern of interaction for several months, Karl sat me down after she moved out and spelled out to me what had become so obvious to him:

> *I think she's baiting you into a trap. She's doing things intentionally designed to make you mad and get you to explode. When you do, you make yourself look terrible, and you allow her to play the role of your victim. I don't think she's sincere in wanting to work on your marriage. And I think she is trying to make you look so bad that she has the perfect excuse to leave. So, here's how*

we're going to find out whether she's sincere.

I want you to go out into the hall and stand on the outside of my office door. Pull the door closed, but don't let it latch. Leave it cracked a quarter of an inch. I'll make sure that there is nothing behind the door to keep it from opening. Now, I want you to back up ten steps, take a deep breath, drop your shoulder, and run at the door as hard as you can. Charge the door with all your might, as if you're attacking an enemy.

As I listened to him, I was wondering, *How on earth is this going to test her sincerity?* However, being the literalist that I was, when he finished I said, "Are you kidding? When I hit the door, it will fly right open. I'll run right through it and fall flat on my face." Karl said:

Exactly! The door won't resist you! The door won't fight back. Force needs to meet resistance to have any effect. The same principle holds in an argument. If she sincerely wants to fix the problem, when she sees that you aren't fighting, she will stop fighting too. If my theory is right and she's not sincere, she'll keep pushing harder and harder to get you to react. It will be hard to control yourself, but if you can, you'll learn something very important about your marriage.

We're told from the time we're little kids that we need to stick up for ourselves. Sometimes that's true, but not always. I learned from this experience that this is particularly the case when it comes to personal relationships. If you ever have a disagreement that is escalating toward an argument, the best way to determine whether the other person is sincerely trying to make things better, or just trying to make you mad, is to stop pushing back. If they really want to solve the problem, they will realize that you've stopped fighting, and before long, they will too. If, on the other hand, their real goal is to provoke you to anger so they can make you look bad and thereby justify their position, then they will keep pushing harder and harder to try to get you to react.

I tested Karl's theory the next time my ex-wife and I got together. At first it was very hard to resist the urge to fight back, but I kept at it. The harder she pushed, the more desperate—and the more obvious—her attacks became. Over the span of a couple of hours, it became comical watching her throw herself against the open door again and again. Eventually, she exhausted herself, like a fighter who shadowboxes so long he can't punch anymore. When I reached the point of actually feeling sorry for her, I calmly explained that I didn't want to fight anymore, but I did want to resolve our problems. She never took the olive branch. If she had, we might have been able to fix our problems. Instead, she immediately went back to launching more attacks and provocations. Shortly thereafter, she started divorce proceedings.

Her final attempt to provoke me came months later when she showed up three hours late to sign our divorce papers. We were supposed to meet in the parking lot of a local shopping mall. It was a neutral location that we both knew very well, so, in theory, connecting one last time to end our marriage would be a pretty simple exercise. We would only need five minutes to sign the papers, and that would be the end of it. After waiting in my car an hour past the agreed-upon time, I walked to a pay phone and called her office to see what had happened. She apologized and said she had an emergency to deal with, but she would be there soon. An hour later, I called again. Same story: an "emergency." She promised she was leaving soon and asked me to wait. At about the third hour, a thirty-foot, white limousine pulled up behind my car. A chauffeur, complete with a black cap, got out of the limo and came up to my driver's side door window. He confirmed my name and then said, "Someone would like to see you." I could now see what was coming. I grabbed the divorce papers, got out of the car, and followed the chauffeur around to the back of the limo, where he held the door open and gestured for me to climb in. I got into the limo. The chauffeur started to close the door, but I stopped him, saying, "This will just take a minute."

Across from me sat my soon-to-be ex-wife. She was decked out as if she were about to attend the Academy Awards, wearing what I assumed was borrowed jewelry and sipping champagne. I handed her the papers without saying a word. As I sat there in silence, she made a grand show of putting down her champagne and looking over the papers like a movie star before saying, "These all appear to be in order." I said nothing. She asked for a pen. In silence, I handed her mine.

As she was signing the first of the papers, she said, "You're probably wondering why I brought the limo?" I think she must have been getting frustrated that I wasn't taking the bait, so she decided to prod a bit more. I said nothing. After a moment, she said, "Well, some friends suggested that I bring it to give us privacy, so we could be anonymous and wouldn't be interrupted. The limo was late, or I would have been here on time."

I wanted to get upset about the fact that I'd been kept waiting for three hours because the limo was late. That didn't exactly strike me as an emergency. It also didn't strike me as the truth, but both points were inconsequential. I was so overwhelmed by the absurdity of her excuse that I almost burst out laughing. It was all I could do to bite my tongue. All I could think was, *Wow, she is desperate! Privacy? Privacy! Are you kidding me? Two people sitting in a nondescript Honda in a big parking lot are conspicuous as hell? A big white limo is anonymous?* This would have been hysterical… if it weren't so transparently pathetic.

She signed the papers and handed them back to me. My only response was "Thank you; I'll see to it that these are filed." I got out of the limo and never said another word. Only when I got back to my car did I let myself laugh out loud. By the time I got in my car, I was laughing so hard I had tears rolling down my cheeks. I never knew, nor cared, if she heard me.

That final stunt was the greatest parting gift my

ex-wife could have possibly given me. Sure, she wasted three hours of my day, but she had communicated perfectly who she was, how her mind worked, and how lucky I was to have her out of my life. Thank God she left me! With my misplaced sense of obligation, I don't think I could have left her, and my life would have been ruined because of it.

I never saw her again.

CHAPTER THIRTY-ONE

Lesson No. 24

Sometimes You Just Need to Walk Away

learned during my divorce—and from countless encounters since—that relationships have harsh realities. Whether I am dealing with a girlfriend, ex-wife, friend, co-worker, sibling, parent, or post-adolescent child, there is only so much I can do to impact their behavior.

In some ways there is a great sadness to this reality that I can't ignore. I can't make others be honest or tell the truth. I can't make them be fair or decent, live up to my moral standards, or even meet me halfway. I can't make them work toward a common goal or be true to their word. I can't make them stop trying to control me. I can't make them love me or treat me with respect. I can't make them stop engaging in abusive or destructive behaviors. I can't make them go into rehab or take responsibility for their actions. I can't make them be rational, see reality, or understand my perspective. I can't make them care, try, think, talk, understand, grow, or learn. Most importantly, I can't make them change.

I can't control other people. They must choose healthy behaviors for themselves. If they don't, I must make a choice to either seek healthier relationships or continue to endure the toxicity of my relationship with them. I've learned that I'm deceiving myself anytime I tell myself things like "If I could just make them see, then they would understand and agree with me, and everything would be okay."

I've learned that if I'm in a relationship with someone whose behavior is causing problems, I have three alternatives. First, I can present my concerns and ask that they change. This usually involves offering suggestions and modeling what I believe to be more appropriate behavior.

Second, I can allow them to independently enjoy the full consequences of their decisions. In this case, I still maintain the relationship, but I limit my participation. This means that I don't bail them out when their behavior lands them in hot water. ("Hot water" can range from an argument with a third party to jail time.) Whatever the consequence of their behavior, I stay out of it and let them work it out alone. I've learned that, contrary to all of their protests and pleas, I'm not doing either of us a favor if I fix their problem. This means that I must do nothing to minimize the consequences of their actions or to facilitate their poor behavior in the future.

Third, I know this sounds cold, but sometimes I

just need to walk away. Some people simply will not change, no matter what. Anytime someone's behavior is genuinely abusive, addictive, destructive, dishonest, illegal, immoral, or violent—and they will neither get help nor immediately discontinue the behavior—I leave.

Leaving any relationship can be a tough call, but I would offer this insight. I've found that when I'm in a relationship with someone who is engaged in these kinds of behaviors, one way or the other, I'm in the pit of Hell with them. (Anyone who has ever lived with an abuser, addict, cheat, crook, or liar knows exactly what I'm talking about.) I've discovered that if two people are in a pit and one finds a way out, that person has two choices: stay down in the pit to keep the other person company, or climb out and try to show the other the way. You have no guarantees that the second approach will work and your partner will follow you to freedom. However, you can guarantee that if you choose the first option, neither one of you will ever see freedom.

It takes two people to make a relationship work, but it only takes one person to destroy it. Both parties have to choose to show up, both have to commit to the relationship, and both have to work to resolve the issues that inevitably arise. I have learned not to fear conflict when it comes. Conflict alone does not destroy a relationship, but failure to resolve conflict does. Yes, it hurts to confront and resolve problems, but if those problems are life-threatening, or if the other person will not join me in trying to resolve them, I'm probably better off alone.

PART FIVE

Lessons I've Learned About Life

CHAPTER THIRTY-TWO

Lesson No. 25

Culture Is King

D uring the first ten years of my career, I spent most of my time working either with small and early-stage businesses or professional services firms. The cultures of these organizations tend to be informal. The only times I interacted with large companies was in support of an audit or business transaction. Consequently, my exposure to the cultures of such firms was quite limited during this period.

In 1994, I had the opportunity to broaden that experience by spending the better part of two years working on the carve-out and merger of MetLife's and Travelers' health insurance businesses. The combination of these two giant divisions created one of the largest healthcare companies in the country—and it gave me a fascinating glimpse into a world I'd never known.

Early in the project, I was invited to a meeting at what was then the main MetLife office, One Madison Avenue in Manhattan. The building was one of the great cathedrals of capitalism, and was affectionately referred to by MetLife offices around the country as "Mother Met." I had never seen anything like it except in the movies. The basement cafeteria was more like a giant food court in a shopping mall. There were rows of elevators. When you got off on a floor, you had to walk past four or five aisles of back-to-back cubes to reach the executive offices along the windows. The aisle intersections were numbered like streets so the mail could reach the right address within the building. The office of the chief financial officer was the biggest office I'd ever seen in my life. It was paneled top to bottom in beautiful mahogany and molding, and there was a conference table in the middle of the room that looked like it could easily seat thirty people. The office had to be sixty to seventy feet long.

We were meeting in the conference room adjacent to the CFO's office. Prior to this meeting I had heard stories about what it was like to work at MetLife. I'd heard that many people were second-, third-, even fourth-generation employees. I'd heard that you were considered to be on probation until you had been there twenty years. However, I'd never heard about the light at the top of the building. In this one particular conference room, there was a giant color photograph of that blinding beacon, clad in glass and gold, shining in broad daylight on the top spire of the building. I gestured to the photograph and asked one of the senior executives standing nearby, "What's this, the eternal flame?"

That flippant remark came out much more

sarcastically than I had intended. Unfortunately, the damage was done. Absolute horror flashed across the faces of all those in attendance. I suddenly felt very alone and realized my inner a**hole had escaped at a most inopportune time. The executive to whom I had addressed my question gave me a very stern look and then rather stiffly replied, "It's the light that *never* goes out! It *is* the beacon of our stability. The only time that light has *ever* been turned off was during air-raid blackouts in World War II."

"Oh!" I said, looking for a rock to crawl under. Luckily, the CFO was a pretty gracious guy. As I tried to blend into the background, he put a hand on my shoulder and said, "Don't worry about it. You're not the first guy to make that mistake." I told him "Thanks" and whispered, "I sure won't make it again."

I had never been exposed to the size, the scale, the history, the pride, the icons, the legends, or the culture of a century-plus-old institution like MetLife. In my ignorance, I had failed to appreciate the mind-set and commitment of the members of that culture or the way that mind-set permeates their thinking and actions. I use this example because it was so stark, but it later dawned on me that I had seen a similar but smaller-scale example of an ancient culture in action before. I hadn't realized it, but I'd seen it in my own family.

Over the years I have discovered that culture is the most powerful force in society. Whether in a family or an organization, culture is the unwritten, unspoken rulebook that determines how the game of life is played.

It's the invisible canvas upon which our lives are painted. It's a million little threads of habit woven together to create the one giant cable that supports our existence. Culture is the cornerstone of our worldview. It defines what we value. It shapes what we do and how we react. Culture is the lens through which everything is filtered.

Culture is so pervasive and systemic, so deeply embedded in our subconscious, that we forget it's even there. We take it for granted, and we incorrectly assume that everyone operates by the same standards. Cultures are deeply rooted, very difficult to challenge, and equally difficult to change. Fighting a culture can be like trying to swim up Niagara Falls.

Not surprisingly, there are two places where I most often encounter a clash of cultures: in my work and in my marriage. I described my rather clumsy initiation into the MetLife culture, but I must also admit that I had an equally clumsy initiation into the culture of my wife's family. Nobody ever told me that when you get married, you also marry the culture of your spouse's family. When you say, "I do," you sign up to contend with the customs, traditions, biases, habits, dysfunctions, and communication styles of that family.

I have, as I think many others have, made the mistake of assuming that the culture of my spouse's family is the same as the culture of my own. It isn't! I started out interacting with my new family the way I interacted with my old. That wasn't a good idea. The traditions and taboos of the first didn't always translate to the second, and some of what was acceptable before was now seen as offensive. Even the most core value of our families differed. My family valued education above all else; Claire's valued athletics. Faith, ethics, community, achievement, and family were all important (sort of), but they were never our social currency.

Although these cultural realities apply equally to a workplace, I find that there are two significant differences. First, where the culture of a family seems to flow from tradition, the culture of a company flows a bit more from the current chief executive. Second, where the roots of a family culture go back to antiquity, the roots of a business go back only to the date of its formation.

Of all the self-inflicted injuries I've experienced, few were more unnecessary than those I inflicted when I ignored the culture of the family or of the organizations of which I was a part. I wish now I had done a better job trying to understand the culture of the groups I was joining before I started engaging with those groups. I wish I had been a better student of people and their patterns; I wish I had been more focused on others than on myself.

Although I acted out of ignorance and immaturity, I was perceived to be acting out of disrespect and arrogance. The unintended message people read in my actions was that I either didn't care about the culture (and hence the people) that I was joining or that I held it (them) in contempt. Neither was true, but since I couldn't address an issue I didn't know I had, I couldn't correct the situation.

The good news I've discovered from these interactions is that culture is constantly evolving—and that I have a choice: I can either work to learn the culture so I can consciously contribute to its evolution, or I can remain unconscious and watch the evolution go on without me. The first option will allow me to take part in shaping the future I want. The second will do little more than allow me to wonder why things never turn out as I plan.

I think I prefer option number one.

CHAPTER THIRTY-THREE

Lesson No. 26

Attitude Is More Important Than Talent

n late '95, I co-founded a software company with two friends. We all had finance or technology backgrounds, and we were all academically accomplished. We had worked together for years and been part of a consulting practice prior to starting our new company. The oldest of us, a guy named Alex, had been my boss at the accounting firm I'd joined out of grad school. Technically Alex was brilliant, but he hated sales, marketing, and dealing with people. His stated condition for joining the business was, "You guys have to deal with all the bullshit; I won't touch it."

Alex had no interest in developing or running a company. All he wanted to do was develop software and be paid what he thought he was worth. He didn't care about what happened to anyone else in our company; he only cared about himself. To his credit, he told us that point-blank, right up front. My other partner and I really should have listened to him.

Alex had been a star athlete in school. He had been on a team that won an NCAA Division I national championship and had been drafted by a pro team. Injuries, however, ended his career before it really got started. You would think a guy like that would understand the concept of teamwork. He didn't.

As the years went by, our responsibilities in the business forced us down different paths. My other partner and I became much more involved in dealing with investors, software analysts, marketing and salespeople, business partners, customers, and employees. We traveled constantly, and our worldview changed as we were increasingly exposed to scores of ideas, cultures, people, problems, and situations we had never experienced before. All the while, Alex sat in his cubicle, in front of his computer screens, and became more technically sophisticated.

Over time, Alex seemed to develop a binary bigotry. He became increasingly rigid. Technology was everything; people were inconsequential. Perhaps that logic allowed him to feel safe, but it also crippled him. He was never able to have a healthy or enduring relationship with a woman, and he maintained a dwindling number of friends. He thought he knew best and other people knew very little. He had no problem eviscerating anyone at any time if he considered that person ignorant or inferior. He was destroying employee morale, poisoning relationships with our customers, and sabotaging our company.

As my relationship with Alex deteriorated, Claire repeatedly pointed out to me that it wasn't Alex who was changing—it was me! She said I had been the same way, but time and tempering had changed me. Alex had become a mirror that reflected for me what I had been. The further I moved away from that mirror, the larger the perspective I got, and the less I liked what I saw. This was a sobering and increasingly embarrassing realization. Coming to appreciate the fact that the behaviors in which Alex and I had both engaged were wildly destructive was a hard lesson for me to learn. But once I learned it, I will never forget it—because I'm reminded of it daily. I see other people in other businesses make the same mistakes all the time!

In the course of my career, I've had the good fortune to work with some really brilliant people from places like Wall Street, Washington, and Silicon Valley. Some of these folks put the objectives of their team above their own wants and desires. Some of them assumed that their wants and desires were the only things that mattered and should be the objectives of their team. The first group was a godsend. The second group was a nightmare.

I used to think that you needed the brightest people you could get on your team and that you should tolerate prima donnas because their genius made them invaluable. I've learned that nothing could be further from the truth. To be successful you need the brightest people you can get—who also have all the required skill sets, understand that they can't do it alone, and appreciate that they need to be part of a team of competent collaborators. The self-centered genius is rarely invaluable and almost always replaceable. The person who is invaluable is the one who can bring out the best in others.

Prima donnas will torpedo you in three ways. First, since they think they're smarter than everybody else (you included), they think that entitles them to do whatever they want. It's hard to move a team forward when one of the team members is trying to push it sideways. Second, they sow resentment in everybody who has to deal with them. They destroy morale and cooperation as people begin to question why the genius is entitled to special treatment when nobody else on the team is. Third, they undercut other people's self-esteem because they're constantly telling anybody who will listen how brilliant they are and how stupid everybody else is.

Which leads to the reason that I allowed Alex (my prima donna) to stay around: fear and a lack of faith in my team and myself. Although I didn't recognize it at the time, I allowed myself to be bullied, and I bought into the bully's bluff that he was better than me as an individual and better than us as a group. The first may or may not be true, but the second never is. It was only when I got mad enough to fight back that I discovered how insignificant was the pain of losing the genius— and how great was the benefit of his departure.

Many people working together will always accomplish greater things, faster, than any one person working alone. Claire likes to help me remember that fact whenever I get too full of myself.

Lesson No. 27

There Are at Least Two Sides to Everything

I never could understand why Alex was so relationally challenged and so antagonistic to other people. Then, fifteen years after I started working with him, his sister told me that he had discovered their mother hanging from a rope in their living room when he was eight years old. He was alone with her dead body for an hour before help arrived.

Our kids had some friends whose parents we casually befriended. One day the husband moved out and filed for divorce. The rumor mill around the school portrayed him as an evil bastard—until it came out that she was a raging alcoholic and had been cheating on him with several other men.

Over the years I've known several guys, personally and professionally, who claimed to be Midas. Everything they touched turned to gold—or so it appeared. Their business acumen was surreal. They were geniuses who made money hand over fist. They had the biggest houses, cars, boats, and vacations imaginable. They were better, smarter, and faster than anybody else—right up until the moment that their fraud, embezzlement, endless borrowing, or lies caught up to them, and their house of cards collapsed.

I've learned over the years that things are rarely as they originally seem…. That if something seems too good—or too bad—to be true, it almost always is…. That one perspective never shows the entire picture…. That there's usually manure at the base of the rose… and that a rose usually rises from the manure.

As I said earlier, human beings are complex. Each of us is a paradox of conflicting emotions and behaviors. We're all capable of holding two completely contradictory positions in our heads at the same time. We're also capable of acting out those contradictions. I've learned to keep this in mind when I hear about two people having a disagreement. If there are two sides to each of us, then there are four sides in play whenever two people get into an argument. I've learned that however compelling the first person's story is, the second person probably has a good one too. I've found it's much better to reserve judgment until I understand and confirm what both of them have to say.

I've also stopped assuming that one party is the saint and the other, the sinner. I've started to assume that there is more to the story than I know and that, however innocent one party appears, that person has probably contributed something to the problem. I know there are monsters among us, that evil exists, and that people are victimized. But I've also learned that black and white doesn't happen as often as I thought it did when I was a kid.

CHAPTER THIRTY-FIVE

Lesson No. 28

Life Is Neither Easy Nor Fair

Prior to September 2, 1945, the date World War II officially ended, I don't think many people in the West subscribed to the theory that life was easy. However, in the decades leading up to September 11, 2001, that changed. Driven in large part by unprecedented economic growth, the rise of a consumer society, and a tsunami of advertising, we slowly embraced the idea that life and everything in it should be easy. We started to accept the notion that if we had to work at anything or work on a relationship, something was wrong with that project, product, or person. We started to believe that the world owed us a living. By 2000, when the stock market was at an all-time high and money was growing on trees, we were completely hooked on the myth of easy. Everybody who came before us just hadn't been doing it right.

The rest of the world was lagging behind because they weren't as smart, or as good, as we were.

Then came 9/11. Then came a decade of war. Then came terrorists under every rock. Then came the Great Recession. Then came national debts that boggle the mind, real unemployment rates from the mid-teens to twenty-plus percent, and political polarization like we've never seen. All are problems with no end in sight. And suddenly, things don't seem so easy any more.

Life is not easy. It never has been, and it never will be. You can listen to all the ads and pundits you want who tell you otherwise, but those words won't change the unpleasant realities of life. Relationships require work. Innocent children die young. Parents lose jobs. Accidents happen. Tyrants exist and must be confronted. Psychopaths don't care. The world doesn't owe you a damn thing. And trying to blame everything on the other guy while completely ignoring your role in creating the mess does nothing to solve the problem; it only exacerbates it.

So as not to be completely pessimistic, I want to acknowledge that everybody has moments when things do fall into place. You just have to remember that those are only moments. Life is fundamentally difficult. You should not expect otherwise, or get mad when the world isn't turning your way. Any time that you spend being mad because of unmet expectations is time you are wasting by being focused on the impact of a problem rather than on the problem's solution.

Now let's talk about fair. In 1984, the *Wall Street*

Journal ran an article about the Harvard Business School Class of 1964. The authors tracked down the top graduates from the MBA program and personally interviewed each of them about their experiences since graduation. For all other members of the '64 class, the *Journal* sent out written surveys with the same questions. The authors collected responses from all but a few of the class members. The response set for one of the questions was particularly interesting. The question was—and I paraphrase—"In your estimation, what is the single greatest determinant of success?" In other words, given all they had seen and experienced during the last twenty years of their career, what did they think determined whether a person would be successful?

Every one of the respondents said one of three things: luck, divine providence, or being in the right place at the right time. The central theme was that you could be the smartest person in the world, but if the breaks didn't come your way, it didn't matter. Conversely, you could be as dumb as a box of rocks, but if you were at the right place at the right time, you could hit it big.

That is a very interesting observation, and it's one that I've seen play out in my own life and in the lives and careers of many others. Hard work and natural ability are absolutely important, but in the final analysis, they alone do not determine success. Providence does.

Let me give you another illustration. If you were born in the US or another Western nation, even if you are in the lowest socioeconomic bracket of your society, the odds are still extremely good that you were born better off, and now live better, than close to 90 percent of the people on the planet. You had *absolutely nothing* to do with that good fortune—it was luck of the draw—and yet it set the stage for your existence. Your survival, education, health, and ability to position yourself for your future were largely determined by the accident of your birth.

So the next time you feel unfairly disadvantaged by a cruel twist of fate or the denial of an object of your desire, remember just how fortunate, how blessed, you really are. Try focusing on everything you've been given that nine out of ten people in the world don't have. That redirection of your attention will help remove the sting of your disappointment. It may also help you remember that the world isn't fair. And that is the point where—if you have any measure of intelligence whatsoever—you are most likely to discover gratitude.

CHAPTER THIRTY-SIX

Lesson No. 29

Success Is a Process, Not an Event

When I made and lost nearly $10 million, I learned that there is no pot of gold at the end of the rainbow. I learned that there is no moment of instant enlightenment in life when all your troubles disappear forever. There is no "happily ever after." There is no moment when you finally "make it." You are never one big win away from everything being permanently okay.

This is not to say that you will not have high points in your life. You absolutely will. People win the lottery. Victories happen. People meet the love of their lives. Dreams become reality. People overcome horrible obstacles, and things improve. However, this doesn't change the fact that life travels in cycles. There are always highs *and* lows. One always follows the other, and each, in its time, comes to an end. When you think of success, I urge you to keep this reality in mind.

Always stay mindful of the cycles of life, and know that it is every bit as possible to succeed in the down-cycles as it is in the up-cycles. You can handle either side of the cycle well, and you can handle either side of the cycle poorly. If you believe success only exists in the peaks of life, you will have forever lost the ability to grow and find benefits in the troughs of life. And as a result you will waste much of your life. Embrace the entire cycle—the entire process—of life, not just part of it. Remember, life goes on in the winter; you just don't see it until spring.

Remember, too, that "finished" only happens when you die…. That perfect is only found in things that you have no control over and can't hope to create, like a sunset…. That nothing is worthless even though you may not see its value right now…. That success, like failure, is only a result. And that results are only milestones. When we reach a milestone, we need to remind ourselves that it isn't our destination but rather a bend in the road, past which the next milestone will come into view. Be sure to celebrate your milestones, but keep them in perspective. Be happy when they point up, but don't lose hope when they point down.

Life is an ultramarathon over the mountains. You can't run this kind of race the way you would run a 100-meter sprint. If you don't manage the *entire* race successfully, you can never obtain the results you hope to achieve.

The secret of success isn't to finish the race—because

one way or the other, the race ends for everybody. My hope for this book is to share ideas for managing both your peaks and valleys successfully—because the real secret is to run the race the right way. You can't reach a good place in life if you take a bad path to get there. You will lose too many people, including yourself, along the way.

CHAPTER THIRTY-SEVEN

Lesson No. 30

You're Only Finished When You're Dead

I think there are two great myths that cause a lot of misery and distort our view of what life is about and when it's "over." The first is the myth of failure; the second is the myth of success.

I believe it was Tony Robbins who first promoted a notion that I wholeheartedly agree with: There is no such thing as failure; there are only results. If you don't get the results you want, try something else and keep plugging away. I also believe that Woody Allen is correct when he says that 90 percent of success is just showing up—over and over and over again.

There have been thousands of times in my life when I haven't gotten the results I wanted. When that happens now, I've learned to do three things: (1) identify what went wrong, fix it, and try again; (2) if you still don't get the results you want, reframe the problem, reimagine the solution, and try something different; and (3) if the first reimagined solution still doesn't work, try others until it becomes evident that it isn't worth it to try anymore.

I try to remember that the only people who never fail are the ones who never try anything outside of their comfort zone. I've learned that success does not equate with brilliance, and failure does not equate with stupidity. The only stupid people are those who never learn from their failures. I've found that failing is a precedent for learning, just as pain is a prerequisite for growth. We're supposed to be disappointed sometimes; we're not supposed to always get what we want: That's how we learn perseverance, dedication, and tenacity. That's how we develop character, ingenuity, creativity, and genius. And that process never stops until the moment we die.

The second myth is the myth of success, completion, or perfection. One form of this myth is believing that you are done, you've finished, or you have arrived. The ultimate embodiment of this myth is becoming a partner, getting the CEO job or corner office, or owning the perfect car, the house, or—as in my case—the yacht you've always wanted. The myth of success is in many ways more insidious than the myth of failure. I've found that while many of us learn to get past our perceived failures, few of us seem to ever really stop whipping ourselves to achieve success. The danger with this myth is that we can obsess so completely over obtaining our dream that we ignore everything else in life.

One of the most tragic examples of this I ever witnessed was the partner who hired me at the accounting firm I worked for years ago. I was attending the annual Christmas party with my date, and we were seated next to this partner and his wife. The mood, even at the outset of the evening, was strained between the two of them, but it rapidly deteriorated as the night went on and she had a few drinks. As I was seated to the immediate left of my boss's wife, I quickly learned the cause for her simmering disgust for her soon-to-be ex-husband. It turned out that shortly after he joined the firm, she had given birth to a daughter. They soon discovered that their child had been born deaf. She was now fifteen, and in all those years, my boss had been so wrapped up in trying to "make partner" that he had never taken the time to learn sign language. He could not communicate with his own child unless others in the family translated.

It has been nearly thirty years since that evening, and I still cringe when I tell the story. The irony of this man's fate was that after his wife left him and took every status symbol he had accumulated, he lost his position at the firm and—I later heard—was financially ruined.

Working for a goal is fine, but I've learned not to do it to the exclusion of all else in my life. It helps to remember that success is fleeting. There is always another physical, emotional, or spiritual hill to climb somewhere.

CHAPTER THIRTY-EIGHT

Lesson No. 31

People Are Your Bottom Line

I'm pretty sure that when most people think about a bottom line they either think about right and wrong or profit and loss. This concept applies to both our personal and professional lives. And I would argue that now, perhaps more than ever before, the gauge for measuring how well you perform in either domain is the quality of your relationships with the people around you.

When a terrorist strikes; on the day your kids are born, graduate, or get married; on the day you bury a parent or a best friend; or on the day you find out that you or someone you love has cancer, money doesn't matter. Sure, you need money to live, but on the most pivotal days of our lives, on the days we suffer real loss, money is *not* what we think about. People are. I've learned that you can have all the wealth in the world, with the ability to do anything you want anytime you want, but if you don't have anyone you care about to do it with, you've got nothing. A life that isn't shared is something less than a life.

At some point we all make a decision that shapes the rest of our life. The decision is this: Are you going to live for yourself, or are you going to live for other people? Are you going to grab everything you can get for yourself, or are you going to put materialism aside and focus on others? I've learned an incredible lesson about the consequences of this decision. The people who opt for the cash often become the saddest, most pathetic, screwed up, miserable individuals I've ever met. And they die that way.

In a prior age—a time when people spent their entire career climbing the corporate ladder—maybe folks could be excused for mistaking the climb itself as being more important than the relationships they developed along the way. But today, where there is no corporate ladder left to climb (I'll explain in a minute), that kind of thinking is not only wrong . . . it's suicidal!

So what do I mean when I say there is "no corporate ladder left to climb"? The average length of time that the typical American worker stays with a given employer has been steadily falling for decades. In 2012, the average job tenure was down to about four and a half years. The tenure for upper management and executive positions was about half that. Over the course of their working life, the typical American worker is going to hold anywhere from ten to eighteen different jobs. That means you are going to have to get hired by ten to eighteen different employers, and—for the foreseeable economic future—relationships will be the keys to getting those jobs.

After I'd helped to start and sell my third business, and after I'd found myself repeatedly working with the same people in different organizations, something finally dawned on me: We don't work for corporations anymore. *We work for our network!*

Today, our network of relationships is everything. Our network of trusted friends and colleagues has become what a corporation used to be. Our networks are the organizations that look out for us. They are our collaborators. They help us find and get hired at the next job—it is estimated that ninety to ninety-five percent of all jobs come to us through our relationships! Our networks are the ecosystems in which we now must survive.

If that's the new reality, I want my network to be as strong as it can possibly be. To make my network strong, I need to respect the fact that dependability, trust, honesty, integrity, fairness, loyalty, and competence are the only currencies that networks value.

Notice that competence is last on that list. I learned a long time ago that people never make purely rational decisions. People buy from people they like! In today's economy, we are constantly selling ourselves. If people do not like you, they will not buy you. And you can't take false comfort in the idea that the buyer (your potential employer) may not know you; their network will.

Nothing spreads faster than bad news, and a bad reputation is incredibly hard to repair. You don't want to be a pariah in a world in which reputation and relationship are kings. It's never been more important to cultivate your emotional intelligence than it is today.

As I said at the outset of this book, I've had the benefit of an uncommon career, one in which I've been able to work with hundreds of organizations from across the US and Europe. I never realized this starting out, but I know now that the people I've met along the way have been some of the greatest blessings of my life. My clients and co-workers are not just my network; many of them have become my extended family.

My great-uncle, who once headed up a major financial institution, told me right after I graduated from college, "If you ever forget that business is all about people, your life won't be worth living." Over time I came to realize how right he was. I also came to realize something else: on the last day of your life, the only things that are going to matter are the number of people you have loved and the number of people you have been loved by. I honestly believe that if I can keep those two things in mind, my network *and* my bottom line will take care of themselves.

Lesson No. 32

All That Matters Is Your Story

I believe this may be the most important lesson I've learned about life, because it encompasses every other lesson I've shared in this book. I've discovered it applies equally to my personal and professional life, and it has huge implications for my relationships with people. To illustrate this idea, I'd like to share two stories—one business-related, one personal—that I found extremely educational.

Gordon's Day of Infamy

Throughout the fall of '99, we prepared our software company for a major fundraising round. On Tuesday, December 7, we kicked off the Wall Street leg of our road show. Road shows are the business equivalent of the Death March on Bataan. You travel coast to coast across the US (and sometimes Europe) in a week. You talk to everybody you can who has money and who might be willing to invest in your business. It's not uncommon to hit two or three cities in a day or to have up to ten meetings a day with different groups. You give the same pitch so many times you say it in your sleep. After fifty or so deliveries, you can't stand the sound of your own voice. You work twenty-plus-hour days, you don't get any sleep, and you get sick afterward. In the past, I'd always played backup on road shows. This time I took the lead.

We had started this road show on the Thursday before, warming up our act in San Diego, Los Angeles, Silicon Valley, San Francisco, Minneapolis, and Chicago. Now we were in Manhattan for a couple of days. Our investment bankers handled the schedule; I just did the dog and pony show when they introduced me. The first stop of the day was the 38th floor of the old Donaldson, Lufkin & Jenrette (DLJ) building at 277 Park Avenue.

The meeting was to start at 9:30 AM. This happened to coincide with the opening bell on Wall Street. At about 9:20, we were escorted into the money manager's office. The guy was an oversized Gordon Gekko— probably 6'3", 330 pounds, late thirties, jet-black hair that was completely slicked back, a five-thousand-dollar suit, designer silk suspenders, a custom shirt with French cuffs, diamond cufflinks and rings, and the biggest chunk of gold for a wristwatch I've ever seen. His very being was a celebration of wealth. He told us to set up our laptop for the presentation on a small conference table that was directly across from two large video monitors, which he used to track the market.

Our host (I'll call him Gordon) asked for a moment before we started. He picked up the phone and told the guy on the other end—his trader, I assumed—"Short five million shares of Yahoo! at the open." For those not familiar with the parlance of Wall Street, he had just placed a very large bet that shares of Yahoo! would go down in price. This would be the worst bet I ever saw anyone make.

When Gordon put down the phone, it was about 9:28. Our investment banker made the introductions and gave a little background about our company. He told Gordon how much we were trying to raise and what we already had committed. At about 9:35, he turned the floor over to me; I would speak for the next twenty minutes, leaving us five minutes for questions at the end.

Since the moment the market opened at 9:30, Gordon's eyes had been glued to his monitor. When I launched into my spiel, I thought he would pay attention to me. He didn't. He had a problem that was getting worse by the second. Yahoo! closed the day before at $70.20 per share. The stock had opened up, and it kept climbing. By 9:35, when I started talking, it was over $73. Gordon never took his eyes off his screens.

By 9:40, Yahoo! shares were trading around $77, and Gordon was starting to sweat. Around 9:45, he grabbed his phone and told the guy on the other end to "cover the Yahoo! short." (That order was to hedge his bet in the other direction, an attempt to limit their loss.) I glanced over at his screen around 9:50 to see what was happening. The price was nearing $80. Gordon had become a tropical rain forest. He was perspiring so much I thought he was going to have a heart attack. He had lost about $50 million in the last twenty minutes. I felt sick, and it wasn't even my money!

At this point, I realized that my presentation was a waste of time. He was completely distracted—and rightfully so. I finally said, "Hey, this obviously isn't a good time. We'll let you go." He quickly turned, looked right at me, and said, "No, no. This is great. Keep going. I'm fine." I went back to my story, and he went back to losing money. His face grew beet red. The veins in his neck started to bulge. A moment later he picked up the phone again, much more excited this time, screaming, "Cover the damn short! Let me know when it's done." I offered again to stop the presentation. He again encouraged me to finish.

I wrapped up at 9:55, certain that the last half hour had been a complete waste of time—which is why the feedback I got from him at the end of my pitch was the last thing I expected:

> *You have an incredible story! I love the way you're thinking. I've covered business intelligence software for years, and everyone in the space says the same thing: "Make better decisions faster." They tell you what, but never how or why they do it. The result is that nobody really believes their value*

proposition, and it's a tough sell. You're the first guy I've ever heard clearly explain how you were going to make better decisions faster and why it was going to make a difference. Your customers are going to get that story and believe your value prop. I know your bankers. I know they've confirmed that you do what you say. It won't be long before you guys get acquired. I'm in for a million.

I couldn't believe he was going to invest. I also couldn't believe that our story was the one thing that got through to him in the middle of his financial meltdown. That wasn't the first time I had heard from investors about the power of the story and the inconsequence of the technology—but it was the first time that I fully understood what they were talking about.

By the way, Gordon proved to be true to his word. He gave us a million dollars for our funding round. The Yahoo! stock price bounced around that day after starting off like a Saturn V rocket, but still closed at $87—up almost 24 percent! I have no idea where, when, or if Gordon ever covered his short. In August 2000, DLJ was acquired. Just over two years later, our company was acquired too.

Allie Moves Albuquerque

In 2004 I co-founded a mentoring program. It was originally intended for schools, but in late '09 it was adapted to help families dealing with addictions and mental illness. The idea was to capture the lessons that people had learned the hard way and pass them on to kids (and later families) who were coming down the road behind them.

The program used an online software application designed to allow thousands of people from all around the world, most of whom would never even meet, to write a book together. The software used an interview process to trace the lifecycle of the human condition, step by step, from cradle to grave. That interview was crafted over a period of two years by a group of about fifty very accomplished professionals (we had a former cabinet secretary, a Pulitzer Prize winner, a Surgeon General, educators, business leaders, artists, and more) who volunteered their time. The purpose of the interview was to gather eyewitness accounts, not opinions. So, at each step of the lifecycle there was a "topic" (topics were things like going to college or becoming a parent), and each of these topics had two sets of questions. The first set of questions dealt with "What happened?" and the second asked, "What did you learn from it?"

In essence, we provided the outline for the book, and the participants, who selected which questions they would answer, provided the details. Once we received all the contributions, we could push a button and compile all the answers into a manuscript. We would then turn the manuscript into a paperback book and give a copy to each of the people who had participated in the project.

Those of us involved in creating the program

thought the value would come at the end, in the information we compiled for the book. We completely missed the fact that the true magic happened in the middle—in the human interaction of sharing stories. This is what was so important—and so life changing.

The first time we tested the program, in 2006, we paired sixth-graders with mentors whom the kids would interview. The mentor could be anyone other than one of their parents, but for safety concerns the parent had to approve the mentor and monitor the relationship. For obvious reasons, a lot of grandparents were selected. The project lasted about ten weeks. During the first test, we were getting great reviews, but nothing prepared us for what happened at the end: The kids went nuts when we gave them their books, and their parents and teachers were sobbing. Everybody was euphoric. The results were so good we immediately decided to do it again, and I made plans to be there the next time we completed a project.

The next year a little girl, Allie, chose to interview her grandmother, who happened to be dying of cancer. Allie's grandmother died as we were preparing the book for publication. She was only forty-nine. She had given birth to Allie's mom when she was nineteen. She and her husband had worked hard all their lives to get ahead, and she had been diagnosed with cancer just as they were beginning to see daylight at the end of the tunnel. She was gone in a matter of months after her diagnosis. When she passed away, the sixth-graders voted, and all agreed to dedicate the book to Allie's grandmother.

All the kids knew what was going on with Allie's grandmother, and it had the unexpected effect of taking what was an already introspective process to an even deeper level. The value of life—not just Allie's grandmother's life, but of all their lives—was celebrated. People didn't just talk about what they had done, but how and why they had done it and what they had learned during the process. The participants were no longer merely conducting an interview. They were participating in a dialogue, and in those candid, transparent conversations, bonds were forged that would last a lifetime.

The local CBS affiliate ran a morning show segment on the book the day we gave it to the kids. The *Albuquerque Journal*'s main columnist ran an article a few days later. After the morning show, when we got back to the school, I heard three comments by sixth-graders that I'll never forget. The first came when we asked the kids what they thought of the project: What was good? What was bad? How should we change it? The consensus was "Don't change anything! Just make it longer!" (How many times have you seen kids wanting to do *more* homework?) The next two comments caused every adult in the room to choke up. One girl said, "Now I know that if I have a problem, there are places I can go to find answers. Other people have been there before. I'm not alone." A boy added, "You gave us permission to have conversations we *never* would have had otherwise."

I was speechless for a moment. I couldn't believe

those words had come out of the mouth of an eleven-year-old. Both the morning show anchor and the columnist told me later that they had been in their respective roles for twenty-five-plus years and had covered countless stories, but they had never seen anything like the impact this project had on these kids or their families. They also said few stories had gotten to them as much.

Through these and other experiences, I came to realize that sharing my story is like sharing an X-ray of my heart and mind. When I share what I've done, how I've done it, why I've done it, and what I've learned, I reveal who I am, what I value, and how I think. I find that most people, at a deep level, believe that to know how someone thinks is to know that person. And I've learned this is extremely important for two reasons.

First, to the outside world, your story is you. It's the foundation of your public life and civic intercourse. People know you by what you tell them about yourself. You tell people about yourself through your words *and* your actions, and *together* they become your story. That story is your personal brand. It's the announcement that precedes you into the world.

If your message doesn't convey the ideas that you want or need it to, then you have a problem: your story isn't compelling, and you need to change your message. If, on the other hand, your message does convey the ideas you want it to, but those ideas are not supported by your actions, then you have a larger problem: your story isn't legitimate, and you need to change your behavior.

Remember, the message in a story is always comprised of two parts: your words *and* your actions. This is what I failed to realize when I was twenty-six. I talked about how Karl confronted me on this issue in chapter 12. I was misleading others and deceiving myself about what, and who, I really was. I was saying one thing, but I was actually doing something very different, and I was oblivious to my inconsistency.

I finally learned to watch what I say when I realized that every time I open my mouth, I'm sharing a story with the people around me, and those people will pay attention to what I do next to determine whether I've told them the truth. Most people will initially believe what you tell them. Unless you give them a reason not to, they'll trust you and give you the benefit of the doubt. But sooner or later, they will check to be sure your actions support your words—and if your actions don't support your words, people will stop trusting you. When you lose someone's trust, it's hard to get it back. And when that domino falls, others follow. People will not willingly stay in a relationship with a person they don't trust.

When I failed to appreciate the importance of my story and of maintaining consistency between my words and my actions, I put my credibility, integrity, reputation, and relationships at risk. When I failed to evaluate the consistency of the words and actions of the people around me, I subjected myself to distractions, dysfunctions, and heartaches that were completely unnecessary. In both situations, I was sabotaging my life and my future, and I didn't even realize it! Sadly, I see all kinds of people who regularly make the same mistakes today.

In the first of the two examples I shared above, Gordon liked the ideas that our story conveyed: he found our story compelling. He also trusted that we would deliver on the promises we'd made in that story: he thought we were legitimate. Without buying into both components of the story—without trusting our words and without trusting that our actions would be consistent with our words—he never would have made the investment. He never would have entered into a relationship with us. Both words and actions have to be present for a story to work and for a relationship to endure. In this sense, my story, our stories, are foundational.

The second reason my story is important is because it's the gateway to every relationship I'll ever have. The more compelling and legitimate the story I share, the stronger my relationships will be and the more I can help the people around me. A person's story is compelling when he or she is transparent and authentic. A person's story is legitimate when they do—or at least try to do—what they profess to value and believe.

Through the second of the two illustrations I shared above, I learned a very interesting rule about stories: the more candidly we disclose our mistakes and shortcomings, the more trust and admiration we receive in return from the people to whom we make those disclosures. Candor requires courage and integrity on the part of the person who discloses, and it shows respect for the person to whom the information is disclosed. This becomes a self-reinforcing cycle, and the longer it goes on, the stronger the bonds and relationships that are created between the participants. This rule runs contrary to the fears that keep many of us from being transparent and authentic in the first place. Our expectations, that we will be rejected for our disclosures, are exactly the opposite of this rule, but I've learned our expectations are wrong.

Most of us live in fear that if others knew who we really are, or knew how often or how badly we miss the mark, they would reject us. While this concern is appropriate for a small (but admittedly vocal) minority of self-righteous individuals who have deceived themselves into believing that their mistakes are not as bad as the rest of ours, these people are the exception. They are *not* the rule! I find it invariably comes as a pleasant surprise, and huge relief, when we discover that the vast majority of people *don't* reject us. They don't reject us because they're just like us, and they know it! When the mentors of the sixth-graders admitted to the same struggles that the kids faced, they let those kids know they weren't alone—and that was a game-changer.

As I came to understand this priceless lesson, I began to see that our fears don't protect us from the tiny, unaccepting minority or stop bad things from happening to us. Our fears don't stop us from dying (either figuratively or literally). Our fears stop us from living and connecting with the 98 percent of people on the planet who share our struggles and aspirations. The tragedy of letting fear win is that we lose both a chance for joy in our relationships and the ability to make a positive impact in another's life.

We live in a time in which people have never been more technologically connected, yet more emotionally isolated and alone. We increasingly share facts and trivia while sharing an ever-smaller piece of ourselves. We transact communications, but those transactions don't fundamentally improve the quality of our lives. It may be easier to find cheap gas, but we aren't improving who we are. As the Chinese proverb says, "If you give a man a fish, you feed him for a day. If you teach a man to fish, you feed him for a lifetime." Giving a man a fish is transactional: it's an event. Teaching a man to fish is transformational: it's sharing a story.

In the long run, the value of a transformation is infinitely greater than the value of a transaction. The value of a transaction is limited to the participants. The value of a transformation is infinite because it creates a ripple effect that extends forever. In this sense, my story, our stories, are transformational.

I've discovered that managing my story is the most powerful strategy and the most effective means I have for managing my inner a**hole and for helping those I care about to do the same. That said, I have to craft the story of my life consciously, authentically, and deliberately. I have to focus on including and adhering to the lessons I've shared in this book. I have to keep my actions consistent with my words, and I have to be persistent in my dedication to that effort over the course of my life. I've discovered that I have to cultivate my emotional intelligence carefully because, sadly, it does not happen on its own.

Afterword

As I bring this book to a close, I'd like to summarize a few points and leave you with a few parting thoughts. First, I've tried to be pretty transparent about the fact that I grew up in a family that had serious problems with addiction, mental illness, and enablement. I think such conditions are far more common than most people realize, and I think too many of us deny this reality. If I haven't made it clear before, I will now: I hate these conditions. I've seen the devastation and pain they bring to our lives in the present, and I've seen how they rob us of our future. I think these conditions have what amounts to a black hole at their center—a void that sucks the life out of people, strips them of their capacity for growth, and cultivates within them a sense of negativity and helplessness. I think that mind-set traps people in a living hell and perpetuates the dysfunctional culture.

Second, I think I have demonstrated that I was once trapped in that mind-set. When I tried to escape the dysfunction of my childhood, I only succeeded in creating an even bigger mess. I found that, like a lethal virus, dysfunctional cultures are insidiously resilient and ruthless in pursuit of their self-preservation. But I also learned that these cultures require two things to survive: silence and ignorance. The first is not golden. The second is not bliss. Neither is benevolent. Both are poisonous. Allowing these two things to remain in your life is like allowing cancer to run wild in your body. However, the second you remove silence and ignorance from a dysfunctional ecosystem, it starts to break down.

Third, as badly as I behaved, I didn't act out of malice. I acted out of fear, hurt, frustration, a desire for self-protection (with, admittedly, some desire for revenge), and almost total ignorance of any better way to live. It was only *after* I was forced to admit that what I was doing wasn't working, only *after* I broke my own silence, that I could begin the process of overcoming my ignorance and finding that better way.

Fourth, that "better way" is not necessarily obvious, but it is surprisingly simple. It's not one big thing; it's a composite of several little things, none of which are complex. They're just counterintuitive. They also happen to arise from a very different worldview than the myopic, materialistic, self-centered, consumerist perspective that has become the worldview of much of the western world.

In the last thirty-two chapters, I've shared thirty-two of these counterintuitive principles (or tools) that I discovered the hard way. I've found these tools to be phenomenally effective in breaking the silence and overcoming the ignorance that enable the dysfunctions of addiction and mental illness to thrive. I've also found these tools can be mixed and matched to address many of the interpersonal issues that most of us encounter in our journey through life. These are by no means the *only* tools for dealing with our self, people, relationships, or life. There are certainly other tools for cultivating emotional intelligence that are not included in this book, but the ones that are included should give you a pretty decent start on your toolkit.

Fifth, I've tried to be fairly transparent about the often-unflattering circumstances through which I discovered these principles. I've been as transparent as I have for two reasons: First, if I don't acknowledge what happened, nobody else will be able to learn or benefit from my mistakes, and that—in my opinion—would be a terrible waste of a perfectly good learning experience. Second, if I don't explain where the tools and lessons came from, how could I have any credibility when attempting to share those tools and lessons with others?

I have been far less transparent about the source of these principles. Virtually every one of these ideas is biblical. I came to appreciate these principles in the context of the experiences I've described. But I was introduced to these ideas in the teachings of Jesus Christ and His radical explanation of the Hebrew Bible. I have intentionally withheld this fact because, frankly, I wanted you to keep an open mind about the content. I fear that many people would—just as I did—dismiss these lessons out of hand because their bias against and understanding of Christianity is—through little fault of their own—as completely misdirected and warped as mine was.

I'll talk more about these misunderstandings in a moment, but for now the point I want to make is this: A good tool, is a good tool—regardless of the theology of the craftsman who made it. A hammer, a screwdriver, and a wrench are incredibly useful tools to have in your toolbox. I can't imagine that anybody in their right mind would care if one were made by a Jew, another by a Muslim, and the third by a Hindu. What matters is the efficacy of the tool, not the religious affiliation of its advocate. Similarly, I'm advocating the principles in this book based on common sense and a proven track record (these principles really work), not based on any particular sense of morality.

Now, having said all this, I submit to you the choice I now daily submit to myself: Do I use these tools and master them, or do I ignore them? Do I move forward, or do I stay stuck? Is it better to risk the unknown and seek growth no matter what, or to endure what is and not rock the boat? Do I choose to mentally, emotionally, relationally, and spiritually evolve, or do I choose to become extinct? Do I adapt, or do I die? Do I cultivate something vibrant and alive out of things that are dead, or do I stand around watching the dead stay buried?

Selecting the first alternative to any of these questions has consistently helped me break my cycle of silence and ignorance and put me on track for a better life. Selecting the second has always perpetuated that cycle and prolonged my misery. Selecting the first alternative has led to life, hope, and the next stop on my journey. Selecting the second has left me stuck on the side of the road, broken down in the middle of nowhere. The more evidence I see of the massive consequences that flow from this one decision—this choice to either acknowledge a deficiency and seek to correct it or ignore it and maintain the status quo—the more this choice strikes me as being one of the most fundamental of our lives.

The first lesson of chapter 8—that you can't do anything about a problem you won't admit exists—is the starting point for the thirty-one lessons that follow. The last lesson of chapter 39—that all that matters is your story—is the culminating destination, the point at which you share what you've learned with others and give meaning to what you know. The impact we have on the lives of others can be positive, neutral, or negative—but it can only be positive if we choose the first alternatives to the questions above and share with others what we learn from the resulting experiences.

When we risk transparency, when we share our story and candidly admit our own mistakes, both to ourselves and to those around us, we take the first steps toward our own rebirth today and toward the advancement of others tomorrow. We all make mistakes, and those mistakes cause us to feel isolated. The one thing that breaks that isolation is when we acknowledge that reality. That's when other people come out of the woodwork and share their own similar experiences. That's when we realize we were never alone—we just had our eyes closed.

I started this book with stories about how I came to believe there is a God, about the more emotionally *un*intelligent moves I've made, and about what I've come to believe we are supposed to focus on during our journey on Earth. I've shared these things because I never want to feel the way I think my dad did the day he died. I never want to explain to the God who spoke to me in the pre-dawn hours of November 10, 1983, why I ignored two blatant interventions and continued full-speed down the wrong road.

I never want other people to find themselves in those positions either. And I never want others to get stuck in the same traps I did. However, I do want other people to find the peace, joy, and contentment (all things that by age seventeen I had written off as lost forever) that I began to rediscover when I started selecting the first alternatives to the questions I posed above.

Dealing with the issues I've raised in this book has, regrettably, required that I reference the darker aspects of human behavior more often than the positive ones. I've talked about Hell more often than Heaven. But I've learned that Heaven is every bit as real as Hell and that we can experience at least some part of Heaven right here, right now. All we have to do is *consciously choose* the behaviors that lead to Heaven instead of *unconsciously defaulting* to the behaviors that land us in Hell.

Sure, Hell is going to show up in our lives every now and then, just as our inner a**hole is going to escape every once in a while. But those bad moments can be the exceptions; they do not have to be the norm. We just have to choose to make it that way. That choice *is* within our power. And fully embracing the lessons and principles I've tried to share in this book is the best way I've ever found to turn that choice into a reality.

Returning to my misunderstanding that I briefly referenced a few pages back, I've learned something remarkable about Christianity over the last thirty years: It's *nothing like* what I thought it was. I had to get past the trappings that too often have become the face of the modern church. I had to strip away the pomp, posturing, and pretense because Jesus *never* acted like that. I had to realize that the vocal minority of self-righteous extremists who judge and condemn others are sadly misguided and do not represent Jesus' message. I had to discover that the only people Jesus ever judged or condemned were the self-righteous hypocrites who judged and condemned others. (How ironic that their modern-day successors still don't see that!)

I had to learn that to everyone who acknowledged their mistakes Jesus extended love, grace, compassion, and hope. He basically said to them, "It's okay. We're good. Don't do it again. Let Me help you fix it." And then He told them to treat everyone else the same way He had just treated them! I had to see for myself that the overwhelming majority of the church does exactly what Jesus told them to: silently serve in the background, without condition or fanfare. Only then did I realize that the 2 percent of Christian frauds (who, unfortunately, happen to be the most visible and from whom many of us get our initial impression of Christianity) don't represent either Jesus or the 98 percent of Christians who are the real deal.

When I take away all the nonsense that was added later by people pushing their own agenda, when I look at Jesus' actual message, I see a spectacularly beautiful faith. I see humility, compassion, and a love (as I described it in chapter 16) that seeks the growth and restoration of all humanity, regardless of who they are, what they have done, or what they currently believe. I see a faith that compels me to serve, to forgive, to selflessly and continually give myself away for the benefit of others—whether I know them or not, whether they are my friends or my enemies. I see a way of life that says, "I'm last; you're first. What can I do to help?" I also see an impossibly high bar. And while I know I'll never clear it, I also know that by some miracle I am much closer to clearing it today than I was thirty years ago.

Jesus Christ really does save. I'm not talking about the afterlife right now, because on that topic I can only tell you what I *believe*. I'm talking about the here and now, because this reality is something I actually *know*. The lessons that this uneducated, itinerant handyman from the armpit of ancient Israel—who may well have been the most emotionally intelligent individual who ever lived—taught and the way of living He modeled (in 30 AD, in November '83, and in the thirty years since) *saved me from me!*

I'm grateful beyond words for what He's taught me. I owe Him a debt I will *never* be able to repay. All I can do is share the stories of how I came to appreciate the principles He introduced me to in the hope that somehow, someday, those principles, those lessons, those tools might help somebody else.

Now you know why I wrote this book. And now you know why I'm asking this favor: if you found *anything* in here that helped you, please pass this book along to the next person you see stuck in a ditch on the side of the road struggling with the same issues.

Thanks—and may God bless our journeys.

The End

Acknowledgments

This book would have been impossible without the support and encouragement of a number of people who generously gave their time and assistance to bring this dream to reality. I would very much like to thank them all by acknowledging their full names, but to do so would, I'm afraid, compromise the anonymity that, at least for a while longer, I must try to maintain. So until the day when the protection of innocent third parties is no longer required, I will simply thank them with their first names and take some solace in the fact that they at least know who they are.

To Dan and Brent, thank you for your endless enthusiasm and for pushing me to keep going. To Lynn and Irene, thank you for your brilliant insights and your incredible capacity to see the big picture and point out to me the things that were missing. Thank you as well for keeping me honest. To Kent and Nick, the two finest, most emotionally intelligent pastors and mentors I have ever known, thank you for introducing me to so many of the principles that became the pillars of this book. To Meg and Kristy, thank you for your ability to realize the art that I could only vaguely imagine. To Lisa, thank you for helping me polish the articulation of my thoughts and transform my manuscript into a finished product. To Gary, Ken, and Jim, thank you for being there. And to all the other friends and colleagues who have been with me over the years, thank you for your support and all the things you introduced me to.

I hope every one of you knows how grateful I am for your assistance. I never could have done this without you guys.

Managing
Your Inner A✱✱hole™
Online

Take the "Managing Your
Inner A**Hole Challenge" at:
www.ManagingYourInnerAhole.com

🐦

Follow Me on Twitter:
@BWPrescott
#ManagingYourInnerAhole

---

f

Like Me on Facebook:
Facebook.com/ManagingYourInnerAhole

✉

Or Send Me an Email:
BenWPrescott@gmail.com